First World War
and Army of Occupation
War Diary
France, Belgium and Germany

48 DIVISION
144 Infantry Brigade
Worcestershire Regiment
1/8th Battalion
1 April 1915 - 31 October 1917

WO95/2759/2

The Naval & Military Press Ltd
www.nmarchive.com
Published in association with The National Archives

Published by

The Naval & Military Press Ltd

Unit 10 Ridgewood Industrial Park,

Uckfield, East Sussex,

TN22 5QE England

Tel: +44 (0) 1825 749494

www.naval-military-press.com

www.nmarchive.com

This diary has been reprinted in facsimile from the original. Any imperfections are inevitably reproduced and the quality may fall short of modern type and cartographic standards.

© **Crown Copyright**
Images reproduced by permission of The National Archives, London, England, 2015.

Contents

Document type	Place/Title	Date From	Date To
Heading	WO95/2759-2 1/8 Worcestershire Regt. Apr 1915-Oct 1917		
War Diary		01/04/1915	29/06/1915
War Diary	Burbure	01/07/1915	31/08/1915
War Diary	Bayencourt	01/09/1915	05/09/1915
War Diary	Hebuterne	05/09/1915	14/09/1915
War Diary	Bus	17/09/1915	25/09/1915
War Diary	Hebuterne	29/09/1915	10/10/1915
War Diary	Bus-Les-Artois.	11/10/1915	17/10/1915
War Diary	Hebuterne	19/10/1915	19/10/1915
War Diary	Bus-Les-Artois	27/10/1915	01/11/1915
War Diary	Hebuterne	04/11/1915	09/11/1915
War Diary	Bus-Les-Artois	12/11/1915	19/11/1915
War Diary	Hebuterne	20/11/1915	27/11/1915
War Diary	Bus-Les-Artois	28/11/1915	30/11/1915
War Diary	Bus-Les-Artois P.de.C.	01/12/1915	01/12/1915
War Diary	Hebuterne	06/12/1915	06/12/1915
War Diary	Hebuterne P. de C.	08/12/1915	08/12/1915
War Diary	Bus	14/12/1915	25/12/1915
War Diary	Hebuterne	26/12/1915	26/12/1915
War Diary	Bus	28/12/1915	31/12/1915
Heading	1/8th. Bn Worcester Rgt. Jan Vol X.		
War Diary		01/01/1916	01/01/1916
War Diary	Bus-Les-Artois	01/01/1916	01/01/1916
War Diary	Hebuterne	03/01/1916	03/01/1916
War Diary	Bus	09/01/1916	11/01/1916
War Diary	Hebuterne	15/01/1916	15/01/1916
War Diary	Bus	21/01/1916	23/01/1916
War Diary	Hebuterne	27/01/1916	01/02/1916
War Diary	Bus	02/02/1916	08/02/1916
War Diary	Bienvillers	13/02/1916	13/02/1916
War Diary	Hannescamps	17/02/1916	20/02/1916
War Diary	Souastre	21/02/1916	22/02/1916
War Diary	Hannescamps	25/02/1916	28/02/1916
War Diary	Bus	29/02/1916	29/02/1916
War Diary	Bus-Les-Artois	01/03/1916	01/03/1916
War Diary	Pas de Calais	03/03/1916	03/03/1916
War Diary	Trenches opposite Serre	05/03/1916	05/03/1916
War Diary	Courcelles	15/03/1916	15/03/1916
War Diary	Trenches	19/03/1916	22/03/1916
War Diary	Colin Camps	23/03/1916	04/04/1916
War Diary	Sailly Au Bois	04/04/1916	04/04/1916
War Diary	Hebuterne	08/04/1916	14/04/1916
War Diary	Couin	14/04/1916	20/04/1916
War Diary	Fonquevillers	27/04/1916	01/05/1916
War Diary	Fonquevillers	30/04/1916	01/05/1916
War Diary	Couin	02/05/1916	04/05/1916
War Diary	Beauval	04/05/1916	15/05/1916
War Diary	Couin	16/05/1916	16/05/1916
War Diary	Hebuterne	16/05/1916	24/05/1916

War Diary	Sailly-Au-Bois	24/05/1916	01/06/1916
War Diary	Authie	02/06/1916	02/06/1916
War Diary	Bagneux	04/06/1916	04/06/1916
War Diary	Coulonvillers	04/06/1916	12/06/1916
War Diary	Hem	13/06/1916	13/06/1916
War Diary	Coigneux	14/06/1916	14/06/1916
War Diary	Acheux	14/06/1916	14/06/1916
War Diary	Coigneux	21/06/1916	26/06/1916
War Diary	Coigneux 57 D.J.9.c.	01/07/1916	01/07/1916
War Diary	Mailly-Maillet	01/07/1916	02/07/1916
War Diary	Coigneux	03/07/1916	04/07/1916
War Diary	Colincamps	04/07/1916	07/07/1916
War Diary	Colincamps 57 D.K.29.c	06/07/1916	08/07/1916
War Diary	Coigneux	08/07/1916	11/07/1916
War Diary	Colincamps	12/07/1916	14/07/1916
War Diary	Couin	14/07/1916	14/07/1916
War Diary	Bouzincourt	15/07/1916	26/07/1916
War Diary	Fransu	26/07/1916	26/07/1916
War Diary	Houdencourt	30/07/1916	31/07/1916
War Diary	Fransu	01/08/1916	01/08/1916
War Diary	Cayeux	07/08/1916	10/08/1916
War Diary	Bouzincourt	21/08/1916	21/08/1916
War Diary	Aveluy	22/08/1916	25/08/1916
War Diary	Bouzincourt	26/08/1916	26/08/1916
War Diary	Forceville	27/08/1916	27/08/1916
War Diary	Auchonvillers Trenches	27/08/1916	05/09/1916
War Diary	Huts Bus	06/09/1916	30/09/1916
War Diary	Beaudricourt	01/10/1916	01/10/1916
War Diary	Mondicourt	02/10/1916	09/10/1916
War Diary	Warlincourt	10/10/1916	12/10/1916
War Diary	Souastre	13/10/1916	15/10/1916
War Diary	Trenches N.E. of Hebuterne	16/10/1916	19/10/1916
War Diary	Souastre	20/10/1916	20/10/1916
War Diary	Beaudricourt	21/10/1916	25/10/1916
War Diary	Bresle	25/10/1916	31/10/1916
Heading	War Diary Of 1/8th Worcester Regt. From 1st to 30th Nov 1916 (Vol XX)		
War Diary	Albert (W.28)	01/11/1916	01/11/1916
War Diary	Contalmaison (x 16.d)	02/11/1916	03/11/1916
War Diary	Trenches Le Sars. (M16)	04/11/1916	05/11/1916
War Diary	Le Sars Trenches	05/11/1916	05/11/1916
War Diary	Scotts Redoubt X 21 b	06/11/1916	07/11/1916
War Diary	Trenches (Bazentin)	08/11/1916	10/11/1916
War Diary	Peake Wood X 22 d	11/11/1916	19/11/1916
War Diary	Martin Puich	20/11/1916	24/11/1916
War Diary	Shelter Wood Camp.	25/11/1916	27/11/1916
War Diary	Scotts Redoubt Trench Camp	28/11/1916	30/11/1916
Heading	War Diary of 1/8th Worcestershire Regiment From 1st December 1916 to 31st December 1916 Volume 21		
War Diary	Scotts Redoubt North X 21.b.94	01/12/1916	02/12/1916
War Diary	Le Sars Trenches	03/12/1916	04/12/1916
Miscellaneous	Report on Raid 1/8 Worcs	04/12/1916	04/12/1916
Miscellaneous	Stores Required		
Miscellaneous	Composition of Raiding Party		
Miscellaneous	Orders	28/11/1916	28/11/1916
Miscellaneous	Headquarters 144 Infy Bde	30/11/1916	30/11/1916

Miscellaneous	Scheme For Raid On Enemy Line		
Miscellaneous	144 Inf Bde App "C"	28/11/1916	28/11/1916
War Diary	Le Sars Trenches	04/12/1916	06/12/1916
War Diary	Scotts Red North	07/12/1916	10/12/1916
War Diary	Martin Puich	11/12/1916	12/12/1916
War Diary	Le Sars Trenches	13/12/1916	15/12/1916
War Diary	Mametz Wood Camp	16/12/1916	30/12/1916
War Diary	Baizieux	31/12/1916	31/12/1916
Heading	War Diary of 1/8th Bn Worcestershire Regt From Nov to 31st January 1917 (Volume XXII)		
War Diary	Baisieux	01/01/1917	09/01/1917
War Diary	Doudelainville	10/01/1917	31/01/1917
War Diary	Sophie Trench Herbecourt	01/02/1917	06/02/1917
War Diary	Front Line	07/02/1917	08/02/1917
War Diary	Eclusier	09/02/1917	14/02/1917
War Diary	Cappy	14/02/1917	16/02/1917
War Diary	Herbecourt	17/02/1917	20/02/1917
War Diary	Front Line	21/02/1917	24/02/1917
War Diary	Herbecourt	25/02/1917	25/02/1917
War Diary	Cappy	26/02/1917	28/02/1917
Heading	1/8th Bn Worcestershire Regiment War Diary For March 1917 Volume 24		
War Diary	Cappy	01/03/1917	01/03/1917
War Diary	Trenches Biaches	03/03/1917	07/03/1917
War Diary	Cappy	08/03/1917	12/03/1917
War Diary	Trenches S. of. Biaches	13/03/1917	17/03/1917
War Diary	Achille Valley	18/03/1917	20/03/1917
War Diary	Flaucourt & Herbecourt	21/03/1917	27/03/1917
War Diary	Peronne	27/03/1917	28/03/1917
War Diary	Hamel	29/03/1917	30/03/1917
War Diary	Villers-Faucon	30/03/1917	31/03/1917
Heading	War Diary Of 1/8th Bn. The Worcestershire Regt. From 1/4/14 To 30/4/14 (Vol XXIV)		
War Diary	Villers Faucon	01/04/1917	03/04/1917
War Diary	Tincourt	04/04/1917	05/04/1917
War Diary	Outpost Line between Ronssoy & Hargicourt	05/04/1917	05/04/1917
War Diary	Tincourt	06/04/1917	06/04/1917
War Diary	Villers Faucon	07/04/1917	09/04/1917
War Diary	Templeux Wood	10/04/1917	11/04/1917
War Diary	Villers Faucon	12/04/1917	13/04/1917
War Diary	Tincourt	14/04/1917	15/04/1917
War Diary	Camp near Roisel	16/04/1917	19/04/1917
War Diary	Outpost Line From X Roods F 29 bos to F 11 d.	20/04/1917	21/04/1917
War Diary	Camps E 29 & F 25 a	22/04/1917	25/04/1917
War Diary	Hamel	26/04/1917	27/04/1917
War Diary	K 5 Central	28/04/1917	28/04/1917
War Diary	Outpost Line From AYD to A 29 C	29/04/1917	30/04/1917
Heading	War Diary of 1/8th Bn The Worcestershire Regt 1st May to 31st May 1917 (Vol XXVI)		
War Diary	Map-France 62 C 1/40000 Outpost line from A 7d. to A.29.c	01/05/1917	01/05/1917
War Diary	K5 Central	02/05/1917	02/05/1917
War Diary	Buire J 27	03/05/1917	07/05/1917
War Diary	Map Buire 62c J.27	07/05/1917	12/05/1917
War Diary	Combles Map France 57c 1/40000	13/05/1917	13/05/1917
War Diary	Le Transloy Villers-Au-Flus N.30-0.7	14/05/1917	14/05/1917

War Diary	Velu J.31	15/05/1917	16/05/1917
War Diary	Velu Map France 57c 1/40000 J. 31.	17/05/1917	20/05/1917
War Diary	Louverval Outpost Line D22 C & d to D29c (57c 1/40000)	21/05/1917	21/05/1917
War Diary	Louverval Outpost Line D22 C & d to D29c (57c)	22/05/1917	23/05/1917
War Diary	Outpost Line D22 C & d to D29c	24/05/1917	29/05/1917
War Diary	Velu	30/05/1917	31/05/1917
Heading	War Diary of 1/8th Bn The Worcestershire Regt (T.F.) 1st June to 30th June 1917 (Vol. XXVII)		
War Diary	Velu J 31	01/06/1917	14/06/1917
War Diary	Louverval	14/06/1917	14/06/1917
War Diary	Velu	15/06/1917	24/06/1917
War Diary	Louverval	24/06/1917	30/06/1917
Heading	War Diary of 1/8th Bn Worcestershire Regt. (T.F) From 1st July to 31st July 1917 (Vol XXVIII)		
War Diary	Louverval	01/07/1917	02/07/1917
War Diary	Louverval Fremicourt Achiet-Le-Pert	03/07/1917	03/07/1917
War Diary	Achiet-Le-Petit	04/07/1917	04/07/1917
War Diary	Monchy	04/07/1917	05/07/1917
War Diary	Adinfer	06/07/1917	06/07/1917
War Diary	Monchy	06/07/1917	22/07/1917
War Diary	Poperinghe	23/07/1917	31/07/1917
Heading	War Diary of 1/8th Bn Worcestershire Regt From 1/8/17 to 31/8/17 (Vol XXIX)		
War Diary	Brake Camp	13/08/1917	15/08/1917
War Diary	Reigersburg Camp	16/08/1917	16/08/1917
War Diary	Civilization Farm	17/08/1917	17/08/1917
War Diary	Alberta	18/08/1917	19/08/1917
War Diary	Roobart Camp	01/08/1917	05/08/1917
War Diary	Dambre Camp	06/08/1917	08/08/1917
War Diary	Brake Camp	09/08/1917	12/08/1917
War Diary	Alberta	19/08/1917	20/08/1917
War Diary	Canal Bank	20/08/1917	20/08/1917
War Diary	Reigersburg Camp	21/08/1917	25/08/1917
War Diary	Alberta	25/08/1917	25/08/1917
War Diary	Reigersburg Camp	26/08/1917	26/08/1917
War Diary	Alberta	26/08/1917	26/08/1917
War Diary	Maison du Hibou	27/08/1917	29/08/1917
War Diary	St. Janster Biezen	29/08/1917	31/08/1917
Heading	War Diary Of 1/8th Bn The Worcestershire Regt. T.F. From 1/9/17 to 30/9/17 (Vol XXX)		
War Diary	School Camp (27 N.E. Eqa J9)	01/09/1917	11/09/1917
War Diary	School Camp	12/09/1917	17/09/1917
War Diary	Recques	18/09/1917	30/09/1917
Heading	1/8th Worcestershire Regiment War Diary 1st October-31st October 1917 Volume XXXI		
War Diary	Recques	01/10/1917	01/10/1917
War Diary	Brake Camp	02/10/1917	06/10/1917
War Diary	Canal Bank	07/10/1917	08/10/1917
War Diary	Springfield	09/10/1917	11/10/1917
War Diary	Siege Camp	12/10/1917	12/10/1917
War Diary	Schools Camp	13/10/1917	14/10/1917
War Diary	Penin	15/10/1917	15/10/1917
War Diary	Villers Au Bois	16/10/1917	21/10/1917
War Diary	Cellar Camp	22/10/1917	25/10/1917
War Diary	1/8th Bn the Worcestershire Regt.	26/10/1917	31/10/1917

Miscellaneous Map	8th Bn The Worcestershire Regt. Appendix A1. Poelcappelle	10/10/1917	10/10/1917

WO95/2759-2

1/8 Worcestershire Regt.

Apr 1915 - Oct 1917

Army Form C. 2118.

WAR DIARY
INTELLIGENCE SUMMARY.

1/8th BATTN. THE WORCESTERSHIRE REGT.

(Erase heading not required.)

Instructions regarding War Diaries and Intelligence
Summaries are contained in F. S. Regs., Part II.
and the Staff Manual respectively. Title pages
will be prepared in manuscript.

Place	Date	Hour	Summary of Events and Information	Remarks and references to Appendices
	1915			
	1 April	1.15	Battalion disembarked at BOULOGNE, for service with the Expeditionary Force, strength as follows 27 Officers 912 other ranks.	
		9.p.m	Battalion entrained at PONT DE BRIQUES 5 to 6 proceeding the whole via train fort, machine gun section, 12 wheeled had previously landed at LE HAVRE, strength, 2 Officers, 2 Officers, 84 other ranks 72 horses.	
	2 April	3 am	Battalion detrained at BAVINCHOVE, & proceeded to WLLEGHTERDEGHEM, the South Midland Division having completed its concentration in that neighbourhood, with headquarters at CASSEL	
	3 April		Btn. & other Bns. inspected on parade by the 2nd Army by Gen Sir Horace Smith-Dorrien	
	5 April		Battalion marched to Scrubhum to back billets 1 mile S. of BAILLEUL.	
	6 April		Battalion marched to Ferm NUC of ERQUINGHEM, 1½ M. S.W. of ARMENTIERS, Battalion [...] for familiarisation in trench warfare [...]	
			[...] Coy were allotted to units [...] the Infantry Bgde 24 hrs in the trenches [...] 3 Coy of [...] D to 5 Ryfillers battery C to [...] A to 1st [...] were sent at 7 [...] along the river Lys in support of the Rifles	
	7th		Battalion marched to C FME 1000 yds at NIEPPE on this date the Division took up a section of the French Line, two Battalions of the Brigade being in the

Army Form C. 2118.

WAR DIARY
or
INTELLIGENCE SUMMARY.
(Erase heading not required.)

1/8th BATTN. THE WORCESTERSHIRE REGT.

Place	Date	Hour	Summary of Events and Information	Remarks and references to Appendices
	1915			
	21st M		Remained in Brigade reserve of 144 Divisional reserve, at NIEPPE. The Battalion took up a section of the trench line in the BOIS DE PLOEGSTEERT, relieving the [...]. The Battalion held this sector for 4 days, during which time the enemy were very quiet from the trench [...] on our [...] to N. YPRES. It was thought most [...] the trenches but the Battalion withdrew. We sustained a few casualties during these three days. None were [...]	
	25th M		The Battalion [...] to Brigade reserve at PLOEGSTEERT about 1 mile in rear of the trenches	
	30th M		The remainder of the 1st Division were relieved [...] on [...] returned to [...] the trenches and the whole Battalion marched [...] are now [...] to TOUQUET for a week. WAR 1906	

Wallis R. Pea, Lieut.-Colonel,
Commanding 8th Bn. The Worcestershire Regiment.

Page 3

Army Form C. 2118.

WAR DIARY
of
INTELLIGENCE SUMMARY.
1/8th BATTN. THE WORCESTERSHIRE REGT.

(Erase heading not required.)

Place	Date	Hour	Summary of Events and Information	Remarks and references to Appendices
	1915 5th May		The Battalion went into Divisional Reserve at PONT DE NIEPPE, after occupying the trenches LE TOUQUET & the river WARNAVE for 5 days. Casualties during this period were 1 man killed & 13 wounded. 11 of the latter were wounded by rifle grenades. A patrol (CENTRAL FARM) sent to further rifle grenades falling among men who had arrived round the post, actually found the post empty. The patrol returned to the same trench line.	
	11th May		+ spent several days making a demonstration of being in trenches. Rifle fire + smoke of fires & smudges made it appear as though the line were still occupied, prematurely, in part, MONMOUTH & DESPIERRE FARM about 800 yds in rear was also shelled. About 100 shells fell in all. At 5 A.M. a mine was exploded, presumably in front of MONMOUTH HOUSE by the enemy, doing no damage. The enemy made no attempt to leave his trenches & apparently never intended to carry the inferior of our trench system, but contented themselves with strafing us, or trying to fill us, of doing this. Our strength was total 968 at time, two men killed Lieut J.U. SERJOHE wounded, Lieuts CE DAVIES, SCYTH, wounded (slightly) & remained.	

1577 Wt. W10791/1773 500,000 1/15 D. D. & L. A.D.S.S./Forms/C. 2118.

Page 4.

Army Form C. 2118.

WAR DIARY

INTELLIGENCE SUMMARY.

1/8th BATTN. THE WORCESTERSHIRE REGT.

(Erase heading not required.)

Instructions regarding War Diaries and Intelligence Summaries are contained in F. S. Regs., Part II. and the Staff Manual respectively. Title pages will be prepared in manuscript.

Place	Date	Hour	Summary of Events and Information	Remarks and references to Appendices
	1915.			
	15th		The Battalion went into Brigade Reserve at PLOEGSTEERT. Some trench lives recovered.	
	19th			
	23rd		Battalion went into Div. Reserve at PONT DE NIEPPE. Casualties sustained during tour in the trenches, 2 men killed & 13 wounded. 11 of the latter casualties were due to shells exploding in & about the area, no more peacefully inflicted afterwards. There were also many much further from the reserved.	
	27th		Battalion went into Bde. Reserve at PLOEGSTEERT.	
	31st		H.Q. about 11.30 p.m. in rear of the trenches was shelled, & was to myself hitting a the Sullivan Corner, 2 men were killed, & 1 man killed & 2 wounded of the relieving battalion. Other casualties during this period, 1 man killed & 7 men wounded. Fighting strength 1 Batln., at this date, 27 Officers, 899 Other ranks.	Pimble, Capt. & Adjt. 8/ Worcestershire Regt.

1577 Wt.W10791/1773 500,000 1/15 D. D. & L.   A.D.S.S./Forms/C. 2118.

WAR DIARY

INTELLIGENCE SUMMARY.

1/8th BATTN. THE WORCESTERSHIRE REGT.

Army Form C. 2118.

Place	Date	Hour	Summary of Events and Information	Remarks and references to Appendices
	1915			
	4 June		Battalion received trench-line between LE TOUQUET & the R. WARNAVE. The Battalion encountered trenches being destroyed the following casualties, 1 man killed, 2 Lieut CC DAVIES wounded, moved into Brigade Reserve at HUNTERSTOWN Wood (PLOEGSTEERT WOOD. During this first contact charge had taken place in the memory [south?] the line suffered serious damage but all well instantly to companies. Battalion under the heaviest rain attempts to relieve the number [troops?] in the trench line & return a large proportion in battalion bivouacs & divisional reserve respective. The [Brigade?] held by the 3 brigades was now held by 2, and the whole of the remaining brigade being held in Divisional Reserve. After changes were in Brigade	
	10 June		The Battalion received relief from LE TOUQUET to some distance Mr the R WARNAVE. The 7 SUFFOLK Regt (XIII Div) were attached for instruction in trench warfare & depth & [equipment?] each line 2 Lieut H G CARTER wounded, 2 Lieut W L Cantler slightly wounded (at duty)	
	12 June		The Battalion marched to Divisional Reserve at KORTE PIP.	
	13 June		The Battalion was inspected by Major Gen R Fanshawe, C.B. OBO, in his Divisional command of the 48th Division	
	14 June		The Battalion marched up to neighbourhood of the left of PLOEGSTEERT wood, being in	

Army Form C. 2118.

WAR DIARY
INTELLIGENCE SUMMARY.

1/8th BATTN. THE WORCESTERSHIRE REGT.

(Erase heading not required.)

Instructions regarding War Diaries and Intelligence Summaries are contained in F. S. Regs., Part II. and the Staff Manual respectively. Title pages will be prepared in manuscript.

Place	Date	Hour	Summary of Events and Information	Remarks and references to Appendices
	1915		Bttn. relieved 5th/7th Worc Regt. who were now ready for the trenches between St Yves & the R. Douve. Two companies of the battalion were in the subsidiary line, under the immediate comd. of the O.C. the night, 1 left sector of the Brigade line, & the remaining two at the disposal of the G.O.C.	
	22 June		The Battalion took over the trenches from the Bn 7 Worc. Regt. The front occupied was about 1100 yards, the enemy trenches at this point from 350 to 500 yards off.	
	23 June		A section of King Edwards Horse (XII D.o.H. Mounted Troops) were attached for instruction. Just before midnight, a patrol of 2 Lt. A. Plaistowe + 2 men encountered a German working party, estimated at 20 strong, just outside our wire. The patrol were attacked with grenades but managed to reach our trenches safely. Another patrol of Lt. P.M. Kerwood + 4 men was out about 2am & got further to our left. This was attacked at close range. Lt. Kerwood being hit by a German machine gun, whilst the fire was at once returned to alarm another in our Coy. Lt. Kerwood was killed, & 2 of his patrol wounded. Including the first hours were Lt Kerwood, the enemy commenced shelling our trenches, & also found machine gun & rifle fire as to stop Mellor began to German officers man at our trench close the 5th Battalion whilst Lt Plaistowe was attacked & no killed. He moved thither to the 5th Battalion	

7.

Army Form C. 2118.

WAR DIARY
or
INTELLIGENCE SUMMARY.
(Erase heading not required.)

1/8th BATTN. THE WORCESTERSHIRE REGT.

Place	Date	Hour	Summary of Events and Information	Remarks and references to Appendices
[illegible] (Continued)	1915		Regmt. Reg'l. information which we greatly needed by G.H.Q. No other Germans were actually seen near the attack commenced. The shelling continued for about 30 minutes, & as it was accompanied by infantry & gunners were relieved the enemy attempt in front of their trenches, our men stood to their trenches, & maintained rapid fire to deliver to about 150 to 150 rounds, it differed being grenades were also attempted through the enemy. The night was very misty, & the smoke & self-grown crops between the two lines very long, which facilitated the enemy's movement, & it is also believed that a certain number of the enemy got thro' their trenches, & both into a pollen about 100yds from our hegments to cover the trenches. This attempt the the case may to finish from rifles have been noted close to our line. Our artillery field to the for a bit that half between 12 midnight, 24/25 & 1 A.M.) no guns were in touch owing that between 4 or 5ice. One battery had been relied with us owing to the no head & it was necessary to shoot up the Tue batteries not in the line, in war, & because linked, very held up to fire capable of fire. LCH For Inferdead 1/8 Lt KERWOOD. Although severely wounded himself, attempted to [illegible] body, but could not get him our wire. He gave information as far as	

1577   Wt. W10791/1773   500,000   1/15   D D & L.   A.D.S.S./Forms/C. 2118.

Army Form C. 2118.

WAR DIARY
INTELLIGENCE SUMMARY.
(Erase heading not required.)

1/8th BATTN. THE WORCESTERSHIRE REGT.

Place	Date	Hour	Summary of Events and Information	Remarks and references to Appendices
	1915			
			he returned, & 2nd Lt MYLNE, helping him the while, went out, under fire with Pte JEFF, & brought in his body. No. 1594. L.Cpl T.C. FOX, & No. 2378 Pte R. JEFF has been recommended by the G.O.C. for the D.C.M.	
			An total casualties, chiefly from the enemy's shell fire were. Lt PINKERWOOD, & 2 men killed. 2nd Lt A. PLAYSUNG, & 16 men wounded. The Speakers attached for instruction had 2 men killed, & 2 wounded, whilst in our trenches.	
	28 June		The Battalion handed over the trenches to the 9th XIIth Divn. & marched to BAILLEUL, having left the 3rd Corps, en route to join the 4th Corps, 1st ARMY, now consisting of 1st, 47th, 48th Div	
	29 June 12.30pm		The Battalion was inspected by Lt-Gen Sir W. Pulteney, K.C.B. Cmdg 3rd Corps.	
		9 pm	The Battalion marched to VIEUX BERQUIN, with remainder 1/144th Bde.	
	29 June 8am		The Battalion marched to ROBECQ	
	29 June 9pm		The Battalion arrived at 4th Corps rest billets at BURBURE, remaining in Cpl's Reserve Three Fighting Strength of Battalion at this date, 24 officers, 880 other ranks.	

F Rundle Capt & Adjt.
1/8 W Worcester Regt.

Army Form C. 2118.

WAR DIARY
INTELLIGENCE SUMMARY

1/8th BATTN. THE WORCESTERSHIRE REGT.

(Erase heading not required.)

Instructions regarding War Diaries and Intelligence Summaries are contained in F.S. Regs., Part II. and the Staff Manual respectively. Title pages will be prepared in manuscript.

Place	Date	Hour	Summary of Events and Information	Remarks and references to Appendices
BURBURE	1915 11th July		The battalion remained in Corps Reserve, Co the 4th Corps during this period. Training being proceeded with. Particulars as regards grenade throwing, machine gun firing & bayonet fighting.	
	12th		A general inspection was probably that the strength of other ranks the men held in Territorial battalions would be 800 other ranks to act as in War Establishment. Any of this over a strength there was no prospect of the draft of 100 men which arrived at HAVRE on 29 June being sent to join the battalion.	
	13th		The battalion marched to killed at HESDIGNEUL, 7 miles S.E.	
	13th		March returned to LES BRESIS, 8 miles S-E.	
	14th		On this, the following day, the battalion in common with the remainder of the Brigade carried out beach - digging on a subsidiary line, about 800 yds behind the present line trenches.	
			The battalion marched back to former billets at BURBURE, 15 miles. Lieut. H.P. NEWMAN, 2/Lieut. H.H.G. BENNETT, & Lieut H.S. BENJAMIN joined from Second Line battalion in England.	

WAR DIARY

INTELLIGENCE SUMMARY

(Erase heading not required.) 1/8th BATTN. THE WORCESTERSHIRE REGT.

Army Form C. 2118.

Instructions regarding War Diaries and Intelligence Summaries are contained in F. S. Regs., Part II. and the Staff Manual respectively. Title pages will be prepared in manuscript.

Place	Date	Hour	Summary of Events and Information	Remarks and references to Appendices
	1915			
	11 July	9 pm	The Battalion marched to LILLERS STATION, & entrained for MONDICOURT, where it arrived about 8 next morning, then marched to VILLAGE AU THE, 5 miles. The 48th Div. on this date rejoined the newly formed 3rd Army (Commander Lt. Gen. Sir H. Munro Hamilton) at FROVENT South of the 2nd British line, with Reserve troops between them, the 1st Army. The 3rd Army at present consists of the 7th & 10th Corps. The 48th Div. forms part of the 7th Corps (1st Gen. Sir T D'O Snow) together with the 4th Div. & a Division still training & the new Army.	
			The Battalion was billeted in houses in the BOIS DU WARLUSMONT, about 2 miles S.	
	29 July		of Doulens & the Company who established himself accidently found with the others of the Battalion. The Battalion was relieved from the remainder of the Division by the 8 Guard Brigade (the Company to the S.D.C. 21st Reserve Division (General Duncan?) who was waiting on the line to our Division.	
	30 July		The Battalion took over trenches from the 4th Oxfords & Bucks L.I. immediately E of NEUVE RUE, 2 Coys in trenches, 1 in Support, 1 in Brigade Reserve at	
	31 July		COLUNCAVES S of LILLERS S.W.	

8 Worcestershire Regt.

Army Form C. 2118.

WAR DIARY
or
INTELLIGENCE SUMMARY.

1/8th BATTN. THE WORCESTERSHIRE REGT.

(Erase heading not required.)

Place	Date	Hour	Summary of Events and Information	Remarks and references to Appendices
	1915			
	1 Aug to 7 Aug		During this period the battalion remained in the trenches S-E of HEBUTERNE. The situation was very quiet, & no casualties were sustained. Practically no rifle fire took place, the trenches lying from 500 to 800 yds apart, but there was a certain amount of desultory Artillery each day, on both sides dividing to which no retaliation was offered. Three companies taking up the front line with 2 platoons each, the remainder being in depth behind their own front line. Heavy rain fell on most days, & the trenches, which were very imperfectly drained, was flooded with mud & water, as much as 2 feet deep in many places. The battalion was relieved by the 8th Royal Warwickshire Regiment, & proceeded to Divisional Reserve at BAYENCOURT.	
	7 Aug		Lt-Col. W.K. Pearse, commanding the battalion, was admitted to Hospital, sick, & evacuated to England on 11th inst.	
	9 Aug			
	15 Aug		The battalion re-occupied the same trenches. During the time spent in Divisional Reserve, large working-parties were furnished, to work on all round defences of BAYENCOURT, and various trench lines in the neighbourhood of SAILLY, & the corps line further in rear.	
	23 Aug		The battalion again returned to divisional reserve at BAYENCOURT, on handing over the trenches to 8th Royal Warwickshire Regiment. This tour also was very quiet. A large amount of working	

WAR DIARY

INTELLIGENCE SUMMARY.

Army Form C. 2118.

1/8th BATTN. THE WORCESTERSHIRE REGT.

Place	Date	Hour	Summary of Events and Information	Remarks and references to Appendices
	1915			
	31 Aug.		done in improving the trenches, revetting parapets, building dug outs & traverses, & draining & having communication trenches. Patrols were out most nights, but failed to detect any movements on the part of the enemy, who appeared to remain behind their own trenches, or at work immediately in front of them. We disposed of their working-parties with machine-gun fire, or three occasions. Casualties sustained during this period; 2 men wounded by rifle bullets, of whom one subsequently died. The battalion remained at BAVINCOURT during this period, large working parties on the line or rear of the front trenches being required daily, as before. Fighting strength of the battalion at this date, 27 officers, 803 other ranks. P.E. Whelley, Capt. Adjt. 8th Worcestershire Regt.	

WAR DIARY
INTELLIGENCE SUMMARY

1/8th BATTN. THE WORCESTERSHIRE REGT

Army Form C. 2118.

Instructions regarding War Diaries and Intelligence Summaries are contained in F.S. Regs., Part II. and the Staff Manual respectively. Title pages will be prepared in manuscript.

(Erase heading not required.)

Place	Date	Hour	Summary of Events and Information	Remarks and references to Appendices
BAYENCOURT	1st Sept to 5 Sept 1915		During this period the Battalion remained in Divisional Reserve, the time being fully occupied with working parties on the defence of the village, corps line & communication trenches to the front.	
HEBUTERNE	3 Sept		The Battalion relieved 5th trenches, taking over a slightly-altered line, owing to the 4th Division having moved further to the North. On our right we now held the line between the SERRE & PUISIEUX roads, the 7 WORCESTERSHIRE Regiment being on our right, & the 4 & 6 GLOSTER Regiments on our left. Our dispositions were, 2 companies holding the front trenches, one company in Battalion reserve in dugouts just E of the village, & one company in Brigade Reserve in the KEEP. The four 1 dug outs held 12 days, the companies changing over with one another at intervals of 6 days. A patrol of 6 men under 2 Lieut K.M. MYLNE, attached to 4th 1/4 Germans proceeding to a listening post rather close to our wire, killing one man, whose identity was subsequently recovered by another patrol, which was paid out to the junction He Wing at 60c 66" ... one day and intends along the part. This Lieutenant was given this idea, &c & onto the day & intends along the part. This was clear of a few of a few battens was by no troops for launching an attack in the end	

WAR DIARY

INTELLIGENCE SUMMARY.

Army Form C. 2118.

1/8th BATTN. THE WORCESTERSHIRE REGT.

(Erase heading not required.)

Instructions regarding War Diaries and Intelligence Summaries are contained in F. S. Regs., Part II. and the Staff Manual respectively. Title pages will be prepared in manuscript.

Place	Date	Hour	Summary of Events and Information	Remarks and references to Appendices
	1915			
			At one being made from the trenches in connection with the active operations a Field G.	
			switched in the new feature. The dug in? These guns appeared to interest the enemy	
			considerably & caused a good deal of enfilade shelling on O[?] but of his patrol. A	
			1 Sgt & about 10 other ranks the enemy trench was found & the wire was cut.	
			all preparing fell short on 10 Sept. a patrol of our men started by 2nd Army	
			under Lieut. Clarkston and Sergeant Grenades were thrown including a number of	
			Jam Tin bombs. No damage was caused however.	
	12.5.15		Headquarters & 2 Companies 6th SHROPSHIRE L.I. attacked for instruction in trenches	
			& remained until evening of next day.	
	14.9.15		A patrol of 14 men under 2nd Lieut. G. C. R. PAWSEY & H.S. WILSON went out to lay in	
			wait for a German patrol, in a trench much used by them. They got into position before	
			dark, the patrol being out of sight from the German lines. A party of Germans appeared	
			and on the [?] arriving at [?] the trench from a unexpected direction. 2nd Lt WILSON was	
			killed. A man wounded [?] but [?] provides and [?] mortally inflicted heavy loss on	
			the enemy. About 6th Sep 1915, the fact that the enemy added [?] [?]	
			it would possible to arm their difficulties, what [?] casualties were, after a fight	

Army Form C. 2118.

WAR DIARY
of
INTELLIGENCE SUMMARY.
(Erase heading not required.)

1/8th BATTN. THE WORCESTERSHIRE REGT

Instructions regarding War Diaries and Intelligence Summaries are contained in F. S. Regs, Part II. and the Staff Manual respectively. Title pages will be prepared in manuscript.

Place	Date	Hour	Summary of Events and Information	Remarks and references to Appendices
	1915.			
BUS.	17/9/15		about 25 minutes duration, during which a good many grenades were thrown by both sides, (most of the enemy's falling very short) accompanied by much rifle fire. The attack on this trenches 2Lt WILSON was commanding & intelligence Officer & the enemy attacker till the trenches 2Lt WILSON was commanding & intelligence Officer & the Battalion is at hut villages & are there. The Battalion was relieved by the 5" GLOSTER Regiment (145 Bde) & proceeded to Div. Reserve at BUS-LES-ARTOIS.	
	25/9/15		Notification was received that Lieut C C DAVIES was invalided to England. Sick, having left MARSEILLES on 28 August. With this date the Battalion had been successful in various minor operations on the enemy, & that they suffered but insignificant losses when made to a hostile advance, in conjunction with the general Advance, which commenced this morning. From this date until recently, trenches, the ordinary activities were diminished, & time given to training for the attacks upon TURKEY.	
HEBUTERNE	29/9/11		The Battalion re-occupied the front trench line, as a battery occasion. 2 Lt H.G. WILTER and 2Lt H. Littler. Fd F.G. Smyth at M.G. Lt 26/9/15, 790 other ranks.	

Bewsley Capt. Adjt.
8 Worcestershire Regt

20 Oct 1915

Army Form C. 2118.

WAR DIARY
or
INTELLIGENCE SUMMARY.
(Erase heading not required.)

1/8th BATTN. THE WORCESTERSHIRE REGT.

Place	Date	Hour	Summary of Events and Information	Remarks and references to Appendices
HEBUTERNE	1915. Oct. 1		At this date the Battalion was occupying trenches East of Hebuterne. Situation very quiet.	
	5		Major R. J. Rawson 1/4th Gloucester Regt. was appointed to the temporary command of the Batt. owing to the absence of Lt. Col. Clarke, who was in England on sick leave.	
	10		The Batt. was ordered to take up new dispositions, as soon as accomodation could be made. The line was to be held during the day by one Platoon in each half sector. In each half sector there would also be 1 Platoon in support, 1 in reserve and one in Battalion reserve. By night the front line was to be held by 2 Platoons in each sector. This was arranged partly in view of minimizing casualties in case of a bombardment and partly on account of the approach of winter, the idea being that when a Platoon had spent a day in the trenches it should be relieved from behind.	
Bus-les-Artois	11		The Battalion moved into Divisional Reserve in Bus-les-Artois. Practically the whole of the time was occupied in providing working parties on the Corps line, R.E. working parties, and doing what was possible to improve the billets for the winter. Little or no time was left for training.	

17

Army Form C. 2118.

WAR DIARY
or
INTELLIGENCE SUMMARY.
(Erase heading not required.)

1/8th BATTN. THE WORCESTERSHIRE REGT.

Place	Date	Hour	Summary of Events and Information	Remarks and references to Appendices
BUS-les-Artois	Oct. 16.		Lt. Col. W.K. Clarke resumed command of the Battalion on returning from sick leave.	
	17.		Captain C.R. Whalley, Adjutant of the Battalion was appointed Brigade Major to the 144th Infantry Brigade, vice Major Haigh appointed to a command. Lieut. J.J. Stote appointed Adjutant, provisionally. 8 days relief commenced.	
HEBUTERNE	19.		The Battalion occupied the trenches T.8 Hebuterne. C. Company of the 9th Royal Irish Fusiliers under Capt. Scott, was attached to the Batt. for instruction until the 25th. This tour in the trenches was the quietest yet experienced not a single casualty occurring. A good deal of work was done towards improving the new accommodation necessary for the redistribution ordered on 10th. On the 25th, 2 Platoons of the left & sect. were moved back into Battn. reserve. The Battalion returned to Divisional reserve at "BUS". A new system of work was started, the whole Battalion working under the R.E. on alternate days, the other days being given up to inspections, improving billets and training, especially in bomb throwing. This system proved better than the old, though very little time was still available for training, owing to bad condition of billets & weather & inspections. The Battalion received its first draft of 25 N.C.O.s & men from 1st reinforcement — Fighting strength of the Battn. 26 Officers 806 other ranks.	
BUS lu Oct	27			
	28			
	31			

J.H. Stote
Lieut & adjt. 8th Worcestershire Regt.

Army Form C. 2118.

WAR DIARY
of
INTELLIGENCE SUMMARY.
(Erase heading not required.)

1/8th BATTN. THE WORCESTERSHIRE REGT.

Place	Date	Hour	Summary of Events and Information	Remarks and references to Appendices
	1915			
Bus-les-Artois	Nov. 1		The Battalion was in Divisional Reserve at Bus-les-Artois.	
HEBUTERNE	4th		The Battalion reoccupied trenches East of Hebuterne under the same arrangements as heretofore since Sept. 5. Situation very quiet. One slight casualty. At this time our moral superiority was very apparent, both guns and machine guns had the upper hand (rifles were very little used), and patrols never met with any resistance.	
	8th			
	9th		2 Lieut C.T. LODGE joined the Battalion from the 1st Entrenching Battalion.	
BUS-LES-ARTOIS	12th		Battalion moved back into Divisional Reserve, Bus-les-Artois. The usual working parties taking practically the whole Battalion were supplied on alternate days. The other days being occupied in inspection, a route march, and training in grenadier work.	
	14th		2 Lieut H.P. BORLASE attached Brigade M.G.O. with effect from 14/10/15.	
	19th		Major R.H.H. CREAK to hospital with nervous debility aggravated by his horse falling upon him during a "test night-alarm".	
HEBUTERNE	20th		Reoccupied trenches as above. C. Coy 19th Royal Irish Rifles attached for instruction until 25th inst, spending 48 hours in the trenches and 48 out in the "JEEP". Line still very quiet, except for intermittent shelling; friendly guns more active.	

WAR DIARY
INTELLIGENCE SUMMARY

Army Form C. 2118.

1/8th BATTN. THE WORCESTERSHIRE REGT.

Place	Date	Hour	Summary of Events and Information	Remarks and references to Appendices
Hebuterne	1915 Nov 26 Cont'd		Casualties. 1 man killed 2 men wounded all by shell fire on the same day. Snow and wintry conditions prevailed. Every precaution taken against frost-bite. Oil pots with dry socks & hot drinks in each trench and boxes with straw in them for sentries. Two days prepared in rear of line to be lengthened and joined so as to connect dead ground. Another planned in centre to provide communication trench forward.	
	27th		The 2nd draft of reinforcements — 2 Lieut R H Church and 20 OR joined the Battalion from the 1st "Entire Swing Battalion". 2 Lieut Field, 8th Essex Bn. attached.	
	28th		Bach to "Div" Reserve at Bus. Working parties as usual, 450 men every other day, our afternoon only available for training.	
	30th		Major T.A.W. How assumed temporary command of the Battalion, Lieut. Col. W.K. Peake having taken command of the Brigade during the absence of Brigadier General Nicholson away on short leave. Fighting strength of Battalion. — 28 officers 802 other ranks (including 55 extra regimental employ).	

M Slater
Lieut & Adjt
8th / Worcestershire Regt.

Army Form C. 2118.

WAR DIARY
INTELLIGENCE SUMMARY.
(Erase heading not required.)

1/8th BATTN. THE WORCESTERSHIRE REGT.

Place	Date	Hour	Summary of Events and Information	Remarks and references to Appendices
	1915			
BUS LES ARTOIS P. de C.	Dec 1.		The Battn was in Divl. Reserve in Bus-les-Artois. Information was received from the A.D.M.S. that the Battn. had, for the month of November, registered the fewest admissions to Field Ambulence of any Battn. in the Division; and that for the past 4 months held the 2nd best record. Working parties, under RE supervision, were found on alternate days. The vacant days being given to cleaning hutt'ts, inspections and training.	
HEBUTERNE	Dec 6.		Reoccupied trenches E of Hebuterne from Hebuterne – Serre Road to Hebuterne – Puisieux Rd the 7th Worc. being on our right and 4th Glouc. on our left as before. The trenches were found to have suffered severely from the continuous wet weather all communication trenches except one being blocked, and a great deal of trench being flooded & the sides collapsed. Revetting was proved to be absolutely indispensable, the only trenches which stood this test were those which had been well revetted. The best revetment seemed to be wire netting with a layer of straight straw underneath and plenty of posts driven into the ground and wired brech at the top. Most of the shelters were flooded and many had collapsed. Owing to these conditions reliefs were shortened by half, companies being relieved every 2 days and platoons	

WAR DIARY
or
INTELLIGENCE SUMMARY.

Army Form C. 2118.

1/8th BATTN. THE WORCESTERSHIRE REGT.

Place	Date	Hour	Summary of Events and Information	Remarks and references to Appendices
	1915			
HEBUTERNE Sec. C.	Dec 6	every 24 hour.	D Coy. 16th Manchesters were attached for instruction for 6 days. Also 2/Lt. A. Gregg 3rd Batt Cheshire Regt for 3 days. Great difficulty was experienced in finding accommodation for officers and men, there being not enough for our own alone; a great many men had to be billeted in buildings with little or no protection from shell fire. There was little rifle fire during this tour, but intermittent shelling. Casualties one killed and one wounded, both by shrapnel.	
BUS.	Dec 14		To Div. Reserve in Bus. les Artois. On alternate days working parties on Corps line, road making, etc took every available man. The other days were employed in cleaning & mending kit & clothing, unspectious and training in grenades & wire breaking.	
	Dec 22		Reoccupied trenches as before (in Dec 6.) Trenches had become more deteriorated; the right Sub-section occupied by C & D Coys alternately, being cut off entirely from communication by day (the Battn from 1st Entrenching Battn. "2 2nd Lieut" Gilbert joined.	
	1 & 24 Dec 25		Christmas Day was characterised by considerably more than the usual amount of artillery activity on both sides. Sailly being heavily shelled in	

22

Army Form C. 2118.

WAR DIARY
or
INTELLIGENCE SUMMARY.
(Erase heading not required.)

1/8th BATTN. THE WORCESTERSHIRE REGT.

Place	Date	Hour	Summary of Events and Information	Remarks and references to Appendices
HEBUTERNE	1915			
	Dec 26		the evening. This tour was very quiet from the infantry point of view, chiefly due to the bad conditions of the trenches.	
BUS.	Dec 26		The 3rd draft of reinforcements, 30 OR, joined from 1st entrenching Battn. To Divisional Reserve at BUS. A series of 6 day reliefs was started owing to the wet state of the trenches. The demands for working parties during this tour in reserve were not so great, the men being somewhat exhausted. Sir T.D.O. KCB. The Corps Commander (General Snow) inspected the Battn billets and expressed himself as highly satisfied with all he saw.	
	Dec 31		Fighting strength of the Battn 27 Officers – 804 O.R. including 62 extra regimental employ.	

W. da M. Peebles Lieut Colonel
Commanding 1/8th Batt. The Worcestershire Regt.

48

1/8th Bn Worcester Regt.

Jan

Vol X

Army Form C. 2118.

WAR DIARY
or
INTELLIGENCE SUMMARY.
(Erase heading not required.)

1/8th BATTN. THE WORCESTERSHIRE REGT

Place	Date	Hour	Summary of Events and Information	Remarks and references to Appendices
	1916			
	Jan 1		Extract from the London Gazette Supplement, 1-1-16	
			HONOURS	
			Mentioned in despatches for gallant and distinguished conduct in the Field :	
			Lieut. Colonel W. K. PEAKE ⎫	
			Major F. A. W. HOW. ⎪	
			2nd Lieut (Temp Lieut) C. R. PAWSEY. ⎪ 1/8th Battalion	
			2nd Lieut A. PLAISTOWE ⎬ The	
			2237 C.S.M. Ward, W.E. "D" Company ⎪ Worcestershire	
			421 L. Cpl (A. Sgt.) Wheeler, W.H. "C" Company ⎭ Regiment.	

Army Form C. 2118.

WAR DIARY
or
INTELLIGENCE SUMMARY.
(Erase heading not required.)

1/8th BATTN. THE WORCESTERSHIRE REGT.

Place	Date	Hour	Summary of Events and Information	Remarks and references to Appendices
Bus-les-Artois	1916 JAN. 1		The Battalion was at BUS-LES-ARTOIS, the 144th Inf. Bde. being in Div¹ Reserve, while the 145th Inf. Bde. occupied the trenches.	
HEBUTERNE	3	1.30 PM	Reoccupied the trenches East of HEBUTERNE the dispositions of the Brigade being as before. On this day, 3 hours after relief had taken place, the right trenches occupied by C. Coy, and especially 22 BOURLON and 23 BOUGEAUD, were subjected to a severe shelling for over half an hour, with apparently 77 CM 4.2 and 5.9 shells. This resulted in a casualty list of 7 killed and 8 wounded through the collapse of a large dug-out. The dug-out was constructed by the French before the British occupation of the line and owing to faulty construction failed to withstand two direct hits. The collapse was due to the cross beams not extending far enough beyond the uprights, the absence of wall plates to prevent the frames from shifting, and the longitudinal roof beams being in two sets end to end instead of the length of the dug-out. The beams being of various lengths with the joints distributed over the length of the roof. The second shell hit the end of the central cross beam dislodging it from its supporting upright so that nearly half of the roof collapsed. The remainder of this low	

Army Form C. 2118.

WAR DIARY
or
INTELLIGENCE SUMMARY.
(Erase heading not required.)

Instructions regarding War Diaries and Intelligence Summaries are contained in F. S. Regs., Part II. and the Staff Manual respectively. Title pages will be prepared in manuscript.

1/8th BATTN. THE WORCESTERSHIRE REGT.

Place	Date	Hour	Summary of Events and Information	Remarks and references to Appendices
	1916			
BUS.	JAN.Y 10		was uneventful, hostile's being confined to intermittent shelling. The Battn. relieved 145 Divisional reserve at BUS. LES ARTOIS as before. The G.O.C. in C. General Sir Douglas Haig G.C.B. while passing through the Divisional area came to BUS. and paid an informal visit Battalion in billets. He congratulated the Commanding Officer on his Battalion. 2nd Lieut. T.B. YOUNG joined the Battn. from the 3rd line Depôt.	
	11		2nd Lieuts. L.R. BOMFORD, A.R. SWALLOW, V.R. FOX-SMITH & G.H. SMITH also joined from the 3rd line Depôt. During this tour in reserve 4 whole days were available for training, cleaning and inspecting; only one day being taken up by R.E. working parties. The benefit derived from this was very apparent in the men, who had been observing slight signs of staleness.	
HEBUTERNE	15		Battn. reoccupied trenches as before. The tour was quiet and the weather drier so that the trenches were considerably improved & repaired.	
BUS.	21		The Battn. returned to Div.l Reserve in BUS. as before.	
	22		The 4th Draft of Reinforcements, 137 O.R., joined from the 1st Entrenching Battn. This	

Army Form C. 2118.

WAR DIARY
or
INTELLIGENCE SUMMARY.
(Erase heading not required.)

1/8th BATTN. THE WORCESTERSHIRE REGT.

Place	Date	Hour	Summary of Events and Information	Remarks and references to Appendices
	1916 JAN.			
	23		included 2 1/8 of our own men returned from hospital. 2Lieut J.J. PASKIN, 2Lieut A.L. FIELD 1/8 Bn ESSEX Regt (cyclists) attached and 35 O.R. transferred from the Battn. to the 144th Inf. Bde. M.G. Coy. which was formed on this date. The 4 Maxims, 2 Lindsay wagons and 8 mules were also transferred from the Battn. 4 Lewis machine guns being received in lieu of the Maxims. This tour, with the exception of one day spent on top working parties, was devoted to training in grenade throwing and close order drill and other training.	
HEBUTERNE	27 30		Battn. reoccupied trenches E. of HEBUTERNE under the same conditions as before. In the early hours of this morning a prearranged enterprise was undertaken in conjunction with similar exploits by other Battns of the Brigade. Our object was to burst a sap, with artillery and machine gun cooperation, so as to create a diversion from a larger operation to be undertaken by the 6th Battn Gloucr. Regt, the next Battn but one on our left, in conjunction with the 5th Battn Warwickshire Regt. The last mentioned however found the night too dark and foggy to carry out their object. Our operation succeeded in two parties going out from our right trenches. The first party	

1577 Wt. W10791/1773 500,000 1/15 D. D. & L. A.D.S.S./Forms/C. 2118.

WAR DIARY
or
INTELLIGENCE SUMMARY.
(Erase heading not required.)

Army Form C. 2118.

1/8th BATTN. THE WORCESTERSHIRE REGT.

Place	Date	Hour	Summary of Events and Information	Remarks and references to Appendices
HEBUTERNE	1916 Jan 30		consisting of 2 Lieut J.R. BLAKE and 10 O.R. advanced in line towards the enemy (the second party, Lieut J.P. BATE & 17 O.R. armed with rifle grenades) followed in the same formation at about 20 yds distance, taking a telephone with them. When within rifle grenade range of the gap, both parties lay down and waited for the artillery to open. As the first gun fired the front party rushed forward fuzed two no 5 grenades each and then retired and formed up behind the rear party who promptly fired 18 rifle grenades at the gap and machine gun fire from both flanks immediately opened with rifle and machine gun fire from both flanks but the 2 parties retired in excellent order, marching and using, for direction, a tracing tape which had been laid on the way out. The casualties were sustained from rifle or M.G. fire owing chiefly to the formation of the ground, and were from shells owing to the fact that the enemy artillery did not open until both parties had the reached our trenches through a specially prepared gap in the wire. The explosion was a complete success as it accomplished its purpose by drawing the fire of nearly all the	

Army Form C. 2118.

WAR DIARY
or
INTELLIGENCE SUMMARY.

(Erase heading not required.)

1/8th BATTN. THE WORCESTERSHIRE REGT.

Place	Date	Hour	Summary of Events and Information	Remarks and references to Appendices
	1916			
HEBUTERNE	Jan 30		available enemy guns. The latter also fired in future casualties on the enemy, whose trenches, judging from the noise heard astride the patrol, was waiting, were thought held at this hour. The G.O.C. Division congratulated officers and men on the success of carrying out of this enterprise.	
	31		This tour in trenches was otherwise quiet; casualties 1 killed in the village and wounded in the trenches both by machine gun fire. The weather conditions during this month were fortunately mild; the Battalion did not suffer a single casualty from trenchfoot or frost bite, owing, in the early part of the month at least, to a plentiful supply of long gum boots and careful maintenance of oil-foot where sentries on coming off duty could have their feet rubbed, socks dried and obtain a hot drink, as far as fuel and stores would permit.	
			Fighting Strength of the Battn. 31 Officers 757 O.R. including 6 Officers and 91 O.R. (who are wounded employ, on leave, in JAS etc.)	

Walter K. Peake Lieut.-Colonel,
Commanding 8th Bn. The Worcestershire Regiment.

Army Form C. 2118.

WAR DIARY
or
INTELLIGENCE SUMMARY.
(Erase heading not required.)

1/8th BATT'N. THE WORCESTERSHIRE Regt.

Place	Date 1916	Hour	Summary of Events and Information	Remarks and references to Appendices
	Feb.			
HEBUTERNE	1		The Battalion was holding trenches East of HEBUTERNE, the 7th Batt. Worc. Regt. being on the right and the 4th Batt. Glouc. Regt. on the left.	
BUS	2		The Batt. was relieved by the 5th Batt. Glouc. Regt. and proceed to Divisional reserve at BUS-les-ARTOIS. Most of this tour was devoted to training and inspections, few working parties being required.	
	8.		A report was received from the ADMS stating that this Battalion (bracketed with the 6th Batt Glouc Regt.) had the lowest number of men admitted to Field Ambulance in the Division; the number being 33.	✻ Sheet 57.D FRANCE E 8.
BIENVILLERS	13.		The Batt. marched to Brigade Reserve at BIENVILLERS✻, taking over billets from the 10th Batt. Royal North Lancashire Inf. The 7th Worc. Regt. went into trenches S.E. of HANNESCAMPS; the 6th Glouc Regt into trenches N.E. of HANNESCAMPS, and the 4th Glouc. Batt. into Div'l Reserve in SOUASTRE.	✦ Sheet 57.D FRANCE E 16. and E 22.
HANNESCAMPS	17		The Batt. relieved the 7th Batt. Worc. Regt. in trenches S.E. of HANNESCAMPS, relief being completed by about 10 P.M., The Batt. held trenches 53 – 68 inclusive.	
	18	1.30AM	Enemy started. The 7th Batt. R Warwickshire Regt were holding the trenches on the right and the 4th Glouc. Regt. those on the left	

WAR DIARY or INTELLIGENCE SUMMARY

Army Form C. 2118.

1/8th BATTN. THE WORCESTERSHIRE REGT.

Place	Date	Hour	Summary of Events and Information	Remarks and references to Appendices
HANNESCAMPS	1916 Feb 6/8 (cont)	1.30 AM	The enemy started a heavy bombardment of trenches 50 to 60 (approx), communication trenches, roads and battery positions, using field guns, heavy howitzer and large trench mortar. At about 2 AM the fire was lifted suddenly east from trench 55 and a party of Germans estimated at about 30 rushed the trench. This trench was, owing (principally to the wet weather, completely isolated, the left end being "in the air". The trench was held with 2 sentry posts about 30 yds apart, that on the right having a Lewis automatic rifle which covered a disused sap up which the enemy came. Neither post could see the other. The reliefs for these posts retired to the dug-out in the centre of the trench during the bombardment, keeping a sentry at the door. An unlucky shell pitched in the parados immediately behind the right sentry post — putting the group out of action and enabling the enemy to rush the trench at that spot. They then bombed the dug-out and captured the occupants with the exception of the sentry who was left as dead, his face having been badly	

Army Form C. 2118.

WAR DIARY
or
INTELLIGENCE SUMMARY.
(Erase heading not required.)

1/8th BATTN. THE WORCESTERSHIRE REGT.

Place	Date	Hour	Summary of Events and Information	Remarks and references to Appendices
HANNESCAMPS	Feb. 1916 18 cont^d		cut about by a grenade. They also captured the Lewis rifle. The left post was unable to do much owing to inferiority of numbers (2 men) also to the fact that the enemy had blocked the trench just left of the dug out, also their one man was wounded. The enemy left behind 1 rifle, 1 pair of very large wire cutters, superior to any used by us, a telephone wire running from their trench to ours, and a large number of unexploded grenades. Our casualties were — Our artillery support was very late and weak owing chiefly to the fact that it was not the custom with the Brigade relieved by us, and whose guns were still behind us, to have an officer with the Battⁿ commander. A Reinforcement of 160 NCOs and men arrived from the Base, all except who returned from base hospitals etc., were sent from the 3rd line unit. The Reinforcement was of good quality.	
	20		The Battⁿ went into Div^l Reserve at SOUASTRE being relieved by the 7th Battⁿ Worc. Reg^t.	
SOUASTRE	21			
	22		Lieut-Colonel Garrett commanding the 3/8 Batt. Worc. Reg^t visited the	

WAR DIARY
or
INTELLIGENCE SUMMARY.

Army Form C. 2118.

1/8th BATTN. THE WORCESTERSHIRE REGT.

Place	Date 1916	Hour	Summary of Events and Information	Remarks and references to Appendices
SOUASTRE	Feb. 22		Battalion for 3 days from England. This tour was too short to be really useful, the Battn being in Div reserve during the whole period.	
HANNESCAMPS	25		The Battn returned to the trenches SE of HANNESCAMPS as before. The 4th Glouc. Regt. being on the left, the 6th Glouc Regt in Brigade reserve in BIENVILLERS and the 7th Worc. Regt in Div reserve in SOUASTRE.	
	26		On this day the 144th Inf Bde Commander was informed by the G.O.C 7th Corps that the Division would go into Corps Reserve shortly, the 48th Div having been in the line longer than any other Div in the British Army. Battn informed by 144 Inf Bde that the Div would go into Corps Reserve on March 8th.	
	28		Corps Reserve cancelled and orders received to to hand over the line on the following day to the 10th Batt Royal North Lanc. Fus. This tour in the trenches was extremely quiet, but conditions were very uncomfortable. Two heavy falls of snow were experienced which made the trenches almost impassable. The trenches were held with 2 Platoons of each Coy, the remaining Platoons being in Batt reserve	

WAR DIARY
or
INTELLIGENCE SUMMARY.
(Erase heading not required.)

Army Form C. 2118.

1/8th BATTN. THE WORCESTERSHIRE REGT.

Place	Date	Hour	Summary of Events and Information	Remarks and references to Appendices
HANNESCAMPS	1916 Feb 28 cont		the Platoons in the front line being relieved every 24 hours. This was necessary owing to the fact that in the majority of cases the men in the trenches could not sleep at all. The Brigade was relieved by the 112th Brigade; the Battn being relieved by the 10th Loyal North Lancs Fus, marched to BUS-les-Artois. The Battn was in Billets by 2AM (1st March) This was a very trying experience for the men who came straight out of the trenches after 24 hours with wet feet, the distance being about 8 miles over very bad roads.	
BUS	29		Casualties during the month were Died of wounds 2 Missing 12 Wounded 7 Fighting Strength of Battalion. 30 Officers, 862 OR. including 6 Officers and 107 OR. in extra regt'l employ, Field Ambulances, on leave etc. Walter R. Peake Lieut Colonel Commanding 8th Bn The Worcestershire Regt	

Army Form C. 2118.

WAR DIARY
or
INTELLIGENCE SUMMARY.
(Erase heading not required.)

1/8th BATTN. THE WORCESTERSHIRE REGT.

Place	Date	Hour	Summary of Events and Information	Remarks and references to Appendices
BUS-LES-ARTOIS	1915 MARCH 1		The Battalion was in rest billets in BUS-LES-ARTOIS.	
(2 to 6th)	3		The Battn. marched to COLINCAMPS forming Brigade reserve. (The 144th Bgd. had moved up holding the Southern part of the Divl. line, which extended from our boundary with KFO14 G.R.29.b.7.8 3rd Bgd. from the North to South. Scheme - taking over the new position from the 4th Div.). The system of relief was that 6 Coys went into the line as before. All 4 merged into the line as before. Two Coys in the Battn. first joined the Exp. Force in November 1914 had practised this in Reserve and but Scottish life in the front line contains one in Batt. Reserve and one in Brigade Reserve. Weather conditions being very bad a golden rally was adopted. ("E" Section)	
Trenches offaris SERRE			The Battn. relieved the 7th & 8th Warc. Regt. in the trenches E. of COLINCAMPS K 29 A.B.O. GR.349A being on the right & the 4th Glouc. Regt. to the left. This was one of the worst tours in the trenches the Battn. had yet experienced Heavy snow had fallen on the 4th Inst. this being followed by a rapid thaw, which caused the trenches to fill with half frozen water varying from 1ft to 3ft 6" in depth. This was followed by frost so the	

Army Form C. 2118.

WAR DIARY
or
INTELLIGENCE SUMMARY.

(Erase heading not required.)   1/8th BATTN. THE WORCESTERSHIRE REGT.

Instructions regarding War Diaries and Intelligence Summaries are contained in F. S. Regs., Part II. and the Staff Manual respectively. Title pages will be prepared in manuscript.

Place	Date 1916	Hour	Summary of Events and Information	Remarks and references to Appendices
COURCELLES	March 15th		Battn was relieved by the 7th Worc. and proceeded into Div. Reserve in COURCELLES.	
Serre	19th		The Battn relieved the 7th Worc in the trenches. On this day the Battn received orders to make a raid on the QUADRILATERAL in front of SERRE, the raid was to take place on the night of the 22nd. This was received by the junior officers and men chosen as a great relief. Great preparations were made, the 4 officers and 80 men who were to take part, were sent to SAILLY where a facsimile of the QUADRILATERAL was marked out, and the raid rehearsed by day & night.	
	22nd		On this morning the G.O.C. Div came to see our line, and seeing the bad condition of the trenches and the ground in front, and realizing for the first time the difficulty of making sufficient reconnaissance in the short time given, forbade the Battn to make the raid until a late date.	
COLINCAMPS	23rd		Battn was relieved by 7th Worc Regt and proceeded into Bde Reserve in COLINCAMPS.	
	27th		Battn Relieved the 7th Batt Worc Regt in the trenches. 10 Officers & 40 O.R. of the 12th York & Lancaster Regt. attached for instruction.	
	28th		The Battn furnished a guard of 3 N.C.O's and 12 men for the C. in C.	

Army Form C. 2118.

WAR DIARY
or
INTELLIGENCE SUMMARY.

1/8th BATTN. THE WORCESTERSHIRE REGT.

(Erase heading not required.)

Place	Date	Hour	Summary of Events and Information	Remarks and references to Appendices
	1916			
	Month of Oct 28 29		at advanced G.H.Q. at CHATEAU XALYION BEAUQUESNE. Batt. received 6th draft of reinforcements consisting of 4 7 O.R. This tour in the trenches was heavy in casualties from Minnewefer and rifle grenades. Casualties during the month. Officers :- Capt. E S Jones slightly wounded. O.R. :- Killed 4 Wounded 22	
	31		Fighting Strength of Battn. Officers 33 O.R 836 including 32 in F.A. & 32 extra reg¹ employ.	

R. N. Buckingham
Capt.
Commanding 1/8th Bn. The Worcestershire Regiment.

WAR DIARY
INTELLIGENCE SUMMARY

Army Form C. 2118.

1/8th BATTN. THE WORCESTERSHIRE REGT.

Place	Date	Hour	Summary of Events and Information	Remarks and references to Appendices
COLINCAMPS	1916 Apr. 1		Battalion holding Trenches E of COLINCAMPS (FRANCE 57D K.35.a – K.29.b). During this tour the enemy subjected our trenches to constant shelling & bombardment by minenwerfer, canister bombs & rifle grenades, inflicting considerable casualties. We were unable to make satisfactory retaliation owing to the range being too long for our rifle grenades & owing to shortage of ammunition for our trench mortars. During the relief of our posts, some of which were still isolated, was for the most part a hazardous undertaking, not effected without loss. Unlike last tour, there was no moon during the hours of relief (i.e. after stand down at night), but this had the disadvantage of making the posts harder to find "over the lid." The tour proved, perhaps, the most trying the Battalion had yet performed, despite slight amelioration in weather conditions. The original plan to hold the line for 4 days, was first lengthened to 6 days, & then to 7, while 1 Officer & 4 NCOs per Coy remained an eighth day with the service Battalions who finally relieved us. Total casualties for the tour — 7 killed, 17 wounded.	
	Apr 2		The Battalion was relieved by the 14th & 12th Bns York & Lancaster Regt, & marched	

Army Form C. 2118.

WAR DIARY
or
INTELLIGENCE SUMMARY

(Erase heading not required.)

1/8th BATTN. THE WORCESTERSHIRE REGT

Instructions regarding War Diaries and Intelligence Summaries are contained in F. S. Regs., Part II. and the Staff Manual respectively. Title pages will be prepared in manuscript.

Place	Date	Hour	Summary of Events and Information	Remarks and references to Appendices
	1916			
COLINCAMPS	Apr 3, 4		to billets in COLINCAMPS for the night, moving next day into Brigade Reserve, H.Q. + 2 Coys at SAILLY, 2 Coys at COIGNEUX. (A & D) in huts.	
SAILLY AU BOIS				
HÉBUTERNE	8		The Bn relieved the 7th Bn The Worcestershire Regt in "G" Sector Trenches, S.E. of camp HÉBUTERNE. (France 57D K.17.c. – K.23.d.) the Divisional Cyclist Coy being on our left + 2 companies of the 4th Bn the Gloucestershire Regt (under command of the Commanding Officer of this Battalion) being on our right. Our Batt: line was held by 2 Coys in the firing line and 2 Coys in Support.	
			The 7th draft of Reinforcements was received (9 O.R.)	
COUIN	14		The Bn was relieved by 7th Bn the Worcestershire Regt + moved to COUIN (France 57D J.1.) being in Divisional Reserve. Billets were in huts in the grounds of the chateau. During this fortnight the Battalion was occupied in Coy training, musketry + close order drill. Wet weather hampered training considerably + caused considerable discomfort to all ranks in bivouacs.	
	18		The reinoculation of the Battalion was begun, A & D Coys being completed.	

WAR DIARY
INTELLIGENCE SUMMARY
1/8th BATTN. THE WORCESTERSHIRE REGT

Place	Date	Hour	Summary of Events and Information	Remarks and references to Appendices
COUIN	Apr.26		Lieut G.T. ROSCOE 3rd E. Lancs Div'l Train A.S.C. was attached to the Battalion.	
FONQUEVILLERS	27		Battn relieved the 5th Bn R. Warwickshire Regt in trenches S. of FONQUEVILLERS (S7D, K.3.C.&d.) The 8th Bn R. Warwickshire Regt being on our left and the 4th Bn Glouces-tershire Regt on our right. The line was held by 2 companies, with 1½ companies in support & ½ in reserve.	
	28		The 9th draft of reinforcements was received (S.O.R.) On the whole it was a quiet anniversary tour. The Right Coy were troubled considerably with minenwerfers. The 2 companies not in the front line were shelled with light H.E. in their somewhat open position in the FONQUEVILLERS – HÉBUTERNE Road, the first day. The trenches were in excellent condition, & work was pushed forward on the wire, the dugouts for support companies & the communication trenches on the left.	
	Apr.30/May 1st midnight		A heavy bombardment was opened on to our left by another Division. The enemy opposite us replied on our trenches, with light shrapnel & heavy H.E. Three shells in quick succession fell in the immediate neighbourhood of H.Q. Telephone station. Lieut & Adjt G.J.L. Slater who has just answered a Brigade call, was struck in the side by a large piece of H.E. shell	

WAR DIARY

INTELLIGENCE SUMMARY

1/8th BATTN. THE WORCESTERSHIRE REGT.

Army Form C. 2118.

Place	Date	Hour	Summary of Events and Information	Remarks and references to Appendices
FONQUEVILLERS	1916 Friday May 19	midnight	and died within half an hour. The door of the Sapper Telephone Station was stove in & the entrance blocked with fallen earth, but the Telephonist continued to send messages, though they could have crawled out through a small triangular hole at the foot of the door. The shelling was severe only for a very short time & our front was quiet again within ¾ hour.	
	May 30		Casualties during the month Officers: Killed - 1. O.R. Killed - 3, Wounded 13 Fighting strength of Batt. 33 Officers & 816 other ranks (including 6 officers & 22 O.R. in F.A. Hospitals & 2 Officers & 33 O.R. on extra regimental employ.)	

Walter B. Peck
Lieut.-Colonel,
Commanding 8th Bn. The Worcestershire Regiment.

Army Form C. 2118.

WAR DIARY
or
INTELLIGENCE SUMMARY.
(Erase heading not required.)

1/8th BATTN. THE WORCESTERSHIRE REGT.

Place	Date	Hour	Summary of Events and Information	Remarks and references to Appendices
	1916			
FONQUEVILLERS	May 1		Lt.Colonel W.K. PEAKE Commanding 8th Bn The Worcestershire Regt, wishes to place on record his deep appreciation of the faithful & untiring services rendered to this Battalion by the late Lieut. G.J.L. SLATER during his time as Adjutant. The Commanding Officer is confident that his own grief is shared by all ranks of the Battalion over Lieut. SLATER'S death in action on the night 29/30 April 1916.	
COUIN	May 2		2/Lt W.O.H. WILLIAMS reported for duty from 8th Reserve Battn. Battalion was relieved by 6th Bn R. Warwickshire Regt & moved to COUIN, where 2 nights were spent in the huts.	
	May 4		The Battn marched to BEAUVAL (France 57D G.22.) a distance of 15 miles, in column of route with the rest of the Brigade. The march began at 5 a.m. and was accomplished without a man falling out on the way. The VIII Corps Commander inspected the march at MARIEUX.	
BEAUVAL			The ten days spent at BEAUVAL were occupied in Company Training & route marching, the Battn being prepared on each occasion with full transport & all detachments employed men in attendance.	

Army Form C. 2118.

WAR DIARY
or
INTELLIGENCE SUMMARY

(Erase heading not required.)

8th BATTN. THE WORCESTERSHIRE REGT.

Instructions regarding War Diaries and Intelligence Summaries are contained in F.S. Regs., Part II. and the Staff Manual respectively. Title pages will be prepared in manuscript.

Place	Date	Hour	Summary of Events and Information	Remarks and references to Appendices
BEAUVAL	1916			
	5 May		2/Lt H. R. RYAN-BELL reported for duty from the 8th Reserve Battalion.	
	8 May		The 9th draft of Reinforcements (20 O.R.) arrived.	
	11 May		Re-inoculation continued (2 companies). The Batt. was issued with short magazine Lee Enfield Rifles.	
	15 May		The Batt. marched to Bivouacs at COUIN for the night	
COUIN	16 May		The Batt. relieved the 4th Bn R. Berkshire Regt in G Section, S. of HEBUTERNE. The previous night the 4th Bn R. Berkshire Regt had suffered an intensive bombardment followed by a raid by the enemy in which the Berkshires lost heavily in killed wounded & missing. The trenches of the Right Coy were rendered unrecognisable by the heavy shelling they had received, & exceedingly hard work was needed to restore them to anything like their true shape. During the engagement of enemy was heavily sent up in clearing the scene of the engagement of enemy equipment, & trophies of bullets, shells, & unexploded German grenades. The town was quiet on the whole, though the Right Company was troubled a good deal with rifle grenades.	
HEBUTERNE				

WAR DIARY
or
INTELLIGENCE SUMMARY

1/8th BATTN. THE WORCESTERSHIRE REGT.

Army Form C. 2118.

Place	Date	Hour	Summary of Events and Information	Remarks and references to Appendices
	1916			
HÉBUTERNE	21 May	12.30 a.m.	2/Lieut H.G.C. CARTER & 3984 Pte ROBERTS (C' Coy) (2/Lt Carter's orderly), while visiting No.s 2 & 3 posts, Right Coy, saw a party of 4 or 5 Germans approaching. Mr CARTER at once fired his revolver on them & they retaliated by throwing 2 grenades one of which exploded, wounding Mr CARTER in 4 places in right thigh, groin & Pte Roberts in the stomach and leg. Though suffering severely from his wounds, Mr CARTER made his way to No 3 post to give orders for rifle fire & then struggled back to No. 2 post to do the same, before collapsing from loss of blood. For this gallant achievement he was subsequently (May 27th) awarded the Military Cross. 2/Lt CARTER wounded. O.R. Killed 1, wounded 12.	
	24 May		Bn was relieved by 7th Bn Worcestershire Regt, & moved into Bivouacs at "Point 126" or the DELL. (France 57D J.16. b.8.3.) 1½ miles E.W. of SAILLY-au-BOIS, being in B^de Reserve. Large working parties were found during this tour for trench digging etc by night.	
SAILLY-AU-BOIS	26 May			
	31 May		Exercise carried out with contact patrol aeroplane, exchange of messages etc. Strength of Bn. O.34, O.R. 831, including 4 Off. & 180 O.R. in F.A. & 35 O.R. extra regtl employ & 36 Off. & 180 O.R. in F.A.	

Walter B. Paul
Lieut-Colonel,
Commanding 1/8th Bn. The Worcestershire Regiment

Army Form C. 2118.

WAR DIARY
or
~~INTELLIGENCE SUMMARY~~

(Erase heading not required.)

1/8th BATTN. THE WORCESTERSHIRE REGT.

Place	Date	Hour	Summary of Events and Information	Remarks and references to Appendices
	1916			
SAILLY-AU-BOIS	June 1		Battalion marched from Bivouacs at the Dell (France 57^D NE I.16. & S.3. "Point 126) to Billets at AUTHIE (57^D I.16) en route for a period of rest & training in Corps Reserve. The Bn was relieved at AUTHIE by 8th Bn R. Warwickshire Regt.	
AUTHIE	June 2		Marched to Billets in BAGNEUX & GEZAINCOURT. (France LENS II. 1/100,000 D.3)	
BAGNEUX	June 4		Marched to Billets in Corps Reserve at COULONVILLERS (France LENS II. 1/100,000 A.5) 8 miles E of ABBEVILLE. The march (16 miles) was carried out creditably, no man falling out, despite lack of practice.	
COULONVILLERS			The Battalion was engaged daily in training by Battalion (2 days) by Brigade & by Division (3 days), the 145th Bde joining in the latter. The wet weather hampered operations considerably.	
	June 5th		Capt. L Knowles returned from 48th Div'l School of Instruction, having been engaged in duty as C'ssmm ussdant there since 28/2/16	
	8th		2/Lts S H WILKES, R.C. WAREHAM & C K TURNER reported for duty from the Reserve Battalion	
			2/Lt N E. Chittenden	
	10th		2/Lt R J Hancock } separately reported	

Army Form C. 2118.

WAR DIARY
or
INTELLIGENCE SUMMARY.   8th BATTN. THE WORCESTERSHIRE REGT.
(Erase heading not required.)

Place	Date	Hour	Summary of Events and Information	Remarks and references to Appendices
	1916			
COULONVILLERS	June 10		The whole of 'A' Coy & a number of men (Approx. 50) of 'B' Coy making a total composite Company 200 strong, marched to LOUVENCOURT (2am 57D 1.30) to form a party for unloading at Railhead & for Ration taking. (From 57D A.8)	
	12		The B's less the above 200 marched to Billets at HEM, 2 mls W of DOULLENS. The march was accomplished in the early morning, breakfast being taken by the roadside a mile E. of FIENVILLERS. The same plan was adopted next day. Man ched to COIGNEUX where the night was spent in huts & tents at 57D S.9.C.2.8. Transport & Quartermaster Stores returned to their old grounds in COIN.	
HEM	13		The Remainder of 'B' Coy joined the Coy at LOUVENCOURT, while Headquarters, 'C' Coy & 'D' Coy marched to ACHEUX (57D R.13+14). Headquarters were billeted in the town, the 2 Coys in Huts in ACHEUX woods. Parties were found daily for unloading, unloading, & work on the 7th R.E. Park.	
COIGNEUX ACHEUX	14			
COIGNEUX ACHEUX	21		The Battn marched to COIGNEUX where it reoccupied Bivouacs beside the camp referred to abov. Headquarters were situated at the MAIRIE. A party of 50 from A & B Coys marched to AMPLIER (57D D.27) under 2/Lt Bom- FORD for unloading to whom a party of the Gloucestershire Regt. A	

Army Form C. 2118.

WAR DIARY
or
INTELLIGENCE SUMMARY.
(Erase heading not required.)

8th BATTN. THE WORCESTERSHIRE REGT.

Place	Date	Hour	Summary of Events and Information	Remarks and references to Appendices
COIGNEUX	1916		party of 52 under 2/LT A.R. SWALLOW, drawn from C & D Coys, entrained for FLESSELLES (Lensfor H.Q.6) where they were engaged in unloading Ammunition at Railhead. The party from AMPLIER returned to the Battalion on 28th. That from FLESSELLES on 30th. During this period at COIGNEUX the preparations for the great offensive on the Fourth Army front were rapidly developed. Orders from the Higher Commands were issued daily as to instructions to be issued, and practice training were engaged in by the whole Battalion with enthusiasm. After receipt of orders as to equipment to be worn by all ranks, a new "fighting order" was evolved, to which the men quickly became accustomed. Daily tests of physical training, bayonet fighting, & drifting in fighting order did much to pro- duce queerness of movement in what at first appeared an almost impossible equipment. Games were instituted by way of varying monotony without losing any athletic training. All companies fired the 5 musk grouping practice in the antigens	

WAR DIARY
INTELLIGENCE SUMMARY
8th BATTN. THE WORCESTERSHIRE REGT.

Army Form C. 2118.

Place	Date	Hour	Summary of Events and Information	Remarks and references to Appendices

COIGNEUX — 1916 — June 24

Tube helmet wk sunshine, creditable results. Visual training, fire control, rapid loading etc. In all of this the men shewed a fine enthusiasm & esprit de corps. On 24th began the Alphabetical Calendar commencing at U Day (24th) continuing to Z day (29th). On U Day the C.O. summoned officers took the opportunity to address The Battalion (assembled in 3 sides of a square) on the forthcoming operations, (first explaining them tactically, & then proceeding to remind all ranks of the high importance of a sense of individual discipline & devotion to duty, in which they could look for no higher example in open fighting than that shewn by the Regular Battalions of the Regt. The men's performance to this was clearly indicated in a redoubled keenness over the daily training, and shewing that after 15 months of Trench warfare they were more eager than ever ready to meet the enemy in the open.

June 26 —
Extract from Supplement to London Gazette "mentions in despatches" Major S.H.C. Cook. 90 A/RSM. Heath A. Strength of Bn: Officers 38, O.R. 869. Present with Bn 28 Officers 789 O.R. including attached.

Wallis Peake
Lieut.-Colonel,
Commanding 8th Bn. The Worcestershire Regiment.
R.A.M.C. etc.

Instructions regarding War Diaries and Intelligence
Summaries are contained in F.S. Regs., Part II.
and the Staff Manual respectively. Title pages
will be prepared in manuscript.

INTELLIGENCE SUMMARY.
(Erase heading not required.)

1/8th Bn. the Worcestershire Regiment

Place	Date	Hour	Summary of Events and Information	Remarks and references to Appendices
	1916			
COIGNEUX 57D.Q.5	July 1st		Z day of the great offensive of the Fourth Army. Zero time was notified as 8 a.m. & before 9 a.m. the Battalion was on the march with full transport. The 48th Division was still in Corps Reserve to the VIII Corps, Fourth Army. The 144 Bde & 145 Bde moved into Bivouacs near MAILLY MAILLET (France 57D Q.18.a.). Signs of the Battle that was raging a few miles to the East of us were most distinctly visible — aircraft, the wounded returning on foot & in ambulances, clouds of smoke from the shrapnel barrages on the flanks, & the intense artillery bombardment. The Battalion found the B'de ERS Section.	
	July 2nd		The day in an open field, & the next morning received orders to attack in the AUCHONVILLERS SECTION the night July 2nd/3rd. The 7th Worcs & 6th Gloster were to lead the attack, the 4th Gloster to act as B'de Reserve & the 8th Worcester as Divisional Reserve. The guides accordingly & the troops A&B reached the assembly trenches, when operations were cancelled & the 3 Battalions who had moved up returned to their Bivouac.	
COIGNEUX	July 3rd		Late in the afternoon of the succeeding day the B'des returned to their Bivouacs at COIGNEUX for the night. The news of the first 3 days fighting reaching us by degrees. In the South things were going well, but the VIII Corps has failed to	

INTELLIGENCE SUMMARY

1/8th BATTN. THE WORCESTERSHIRE REGT.

1/8th Bn: The Worcestershire Regt

Place	Date	Hour	Summary of Events and Information	Remarks and references to Appendices
COIGNEUX	July 3rd 1916		57O K.30 – R.9 established the defensive flank aimed at on the SERRE-GRANDCOURT RIDGE. Disappointing though the news at first appeared, it was the unanimous opinion of the higher command, that such has been the concentration of the enemy's infantry & artillery opposite the VIII Corps front, that no other result could have been achieved. That while the Corps had inflicted very heavy casualties on the enemy, it has itself suffered losses, which though of a most extensive nature, were fully compensated for by the heading effect that our offensive has upon the troops opposed to us, thus greatly lightening the task of the British & French Corps engaged South of us. The spirits & morale of the Battalion were therefore in no way impaired by what at first appeared a failure, & all ranks were cheered by the news of the magnificent fighting of the 6th & 8th Bn. R. Warwickshire Regt (attached 4th Division) — the only two Battalions of the 48th Div. so far engaged in the offensive.

Meanwhile (July 1st) the following 8 Officers had reported for duty, 2/Lieuts EDWIN LESLIE BISHOP, 6th Battn., BERNARD HENRY TULLIDGE, 6th Battn, ARTHUR EDWIN JAMES &C/Coy ARTHUR FITZGERALD RAKES, 6th Bn, 6 'B' Coy, RONALD FRANCIS BURN, 5th Batt., 6 'B' Coy, JOHN CHANNING WICKHAM, 4 5 Bn, 6 'D' Coy, GEORGE LUCE DUPRÉ | |

STANLEY CLUTTERBUCK, 8th Reserve Battn,

INTELLIGENCE SUMMARY
or
INTELLIGENCE SUMMARY.
(Erase heading not required.)

1/8 Bn the Worcestershire Regt

Place	Date	Hour	Summary of Events and Information	Remarks and references to Appendices
	1916			
COIGNEUX COLINCAMPS	July 4th July 4		2nd Bn, "C" Coy. HENRY HARDING MILWARD, 3rd Battn. to "A" Coy. The Battalion relieved the 93rd Inf Bde, 31st Div. in the trenches in front of COLIN-CAMPS, remaining till 8th inst. The heavy rain of the previous day had made the trenches in a deplorable state of mud. The great number of gas in and near the trenches caused much work & discomfort, but there was an uneasy feeling that our own troops had the upper hand. The enemy made the fullest retaliation to an perpetual stream of shells; his defences — wire & trenches — were visibly in a terrible plight. The work during this time consisted in bringing the dead, salving equipment between, & repairing the trenches smashed by the enemy's barrage of July 1st, & generally clearing the Battlefield. Patrols went out nightly and as a general feature of the disorganisation & weakened morale of our opponents. On the night July 6/7 we carried out 2 "camouflage raids" at 11 p.m. & 1 a.m., a party from each front Coy going out to within 50 yards of the enemy's parapet & throwing bombs into the trench. This caused him to man his parapet & open rifle & machine gun fire, while our shrapnel fired heavily & him. Our casualties were one man killed in "B" Coy. The 6th Gloster were on our left, the 2nd D. of Wellington's on our right.	57th K.R.C.

Instructions regarding War Diaries and Intelligence Summaries are contained in F.S. Regs., Part II. and the Staff Manual respectively. Title pages will be prepared in manuscript.

INTELLIGENCE SUMMARY.
(Erase heading not required.)

1/8th Bn. The Worcestershire Regt.

Place	Date	Hour	Summary of Events and Information	Remarks and references to Appendices
COLINCAMPS 57.D.K.29.c	July 6th 1916		The following 3 officers reported for duty from 8° Reserve Battalion. 2/Lieuts STUART WILLIAM LEWIS, WILLIAM HARRY GRIFFITHS, FRANK WALDRON.	
	July 7th		The following 2 officers evacuated to Hospital 2/Lieuts STUART WILLIAM LEWIS suffering from shell shock, 2/Lieut FRANK WALDRON suffering from rheumatism. Battalion during the QR. Killed 21 wounded. The Battalion was relieved by 1/7° Bn the Worcestershire Regt., & marched to their	
COIGNEUX	July 8th		bivouacs in COIGNEUX, 57.D J.9.c. The men's feet had suffered considerably from the wet state of the trenches, no gumboots being available. The programme of working parties arranged in the 4 minutes to give the men time to rest	
	July 9th		& recover. Lieut E.C. DAVIES rejoined the Battn., having been evacuated sick to England Aug. 1915.	
	July 10th		2/Lt WALTER RAYMOND BAKER reported for duty from 8° Reserve Battalion and was posted to "B" Coy	
	July 11th		2/Lt REGINALD TOM KEEN similarly reported was posted to "C" Coy	
COLINCAMPS	July 12th		The Battn. relieved returned 1/7° Battn. the Worcestershire Regt in the COLINCAMPS section 57.D.K.29.c. Four days dry weather has improved the trenches & the town was passed in greater comfort than the last. Work was done on the repair of the trenches the 6° Gloster men on our left & the 2° Bn Somerset Light Infantry on our right.	

Instructions regarding War Diaries and Intelligence Summaries are contained in F. S. Regs., Part II. and the Staff Manual respectively. Title pages will be prepared in manuscript.

WAR DIARY
or
INTELLIGENCE SUMMARY.
(Erase heading not required.)

8th Bn. The Worcestershire Regt.

Place	Date	Hour	Summary of Events and Information	Remarks and references to Appendices
COLINCAMPS	1916 July 12th		Draft of reinforcement, 28 O.R., arrived.	
	13th		Draft of reinforcement 19 O.R. arrived. Hitherto of these 2 drafts were brought up to the trenches during the town.	
	14th	3.0 a.m.	A heavy bombardment by the 4th Div. on our right was the beginning of a series of demonstrations during the ensuing 24 hours, the object being to keep the enemy's fire directed on our front while more important operations were proceeding further South. From 3.10 – 3.40 the Battalion discharged a very large quantity of Smoke bombs & "P" bombs, the whole of which was carried to the S.W. wind over the enemy lines, while the artillery bombarded his front line 3.15 – 3.20, lifted to his second line 3.20 – 3.25 to make him think the attack was being launched, then dropped back to his front line 3.25 – 3.30 in the hope of inflicting heavy casualties on the men manning his parapet. His retaliation was considerable though not very bitter, counter bombs & 5.9 shells being chiefly used with some H.E. on burst. Our casualties were 6 men slightly wounded. In the later morning a chance 4.2 shell killed 2/Lt A.S. CLUTTERBUCK & wounded 2/Lt R.L. HANCOCK. Casualties during the Tour Killed 1 officer, 10 O.R. wounded 1 officer, 10 O.R.	

Instructions regarding War Diaries and Intelligence
Summaries are contained in F. S. Regs., Part II.
and the Staff Manual respectively. Title pages
will be prepared in manuscript.

WAR DIARY
INTELLIGENCE SUMMARY.
(Erase heading not required.)

Army Form C. 2118.

1/8th Bn. The Worcestershire Regt.

Place	Date 1916 July	Hour	Summary of Events and Information	Remarks and references to Appendices
COLINCAMPS COUIN BOUZINCOURT	14		Battalion relieved by 16th (City of Cardiff) Battalion The Welsh Regt, 38th Div. Marched to Bivouacs near COUIN on S. side of SAILLY-ST LEGER Road, 57D.J.7.8.9. for the night.	
	15	11 a.m.	Battalion proceeded by Motor Transport to Bivouacs near BOUZINCOURT 57D.V.23	
		8 p.m.	Moving on in the evening to Hutments in BOUZINCOURT village 57D W.8 &c.1.9., half the 144 Bde being in the Trenches, Adv. Bde H.Q. W.18.b.88. The Bde was under orders of 32nd Div. until the morning 16th, when 48th Div. moved to BOUZINCOURT.	
	16.			
	16.		The first Day of the 48th Div's Share in the great offensive. Even was it could hardly be called "hard fighting" [53rd & 56th X2 and 8th SPs E.] not "open warfare". For it chiefly consisted of "sitting" in Trenches lived by O.H.A. The 75 WMCs were in the line with the 4/5 Gloster on their left. 49th Div. to the left of these & 145 Bde to right of 75 WMCs. The 6 5 Gloster were in Bde Reserve, & the 8th Worcesters in Div. Reserve. All ranks looked anxiously to the day when their turn should come to meet the enemy in fair fight after the comparatively tame quietening monotony of Trench Garrison work for 16 months. But the Battalion was disappointed. For the night 19/20 July	

T2134. W. W708-776. 500000. 4/15. Sir J C & S.

INTELLIGENCE SUMMARY.
8th BATTN. THE WORCESTERSHIRE REGT.

(Erase heading not required.)

Instructions regarding War Diaries and Intelligence Summaries are contained in F. S. Regs., Part II. and the Staff Manual respectively. Title pages will be prepared in manscript.

Place	Date	Hour	Summary of Events and Information	Remarks and references to Appendices
BOUZINCOURT	1916 July 1st		a Dressing Station near by, whence they were conveyed to F. Amb. in ALBERT. The full effect of this open poison did not manifest themselves until some 10 to 12 hours afterwards when the men turned violently sick. All question of relieving the 7th Worcs in the Trenches had to be abandoned, only 18 men being fit for duty beyond Transport, Headquarters & the Quarter-Master Details, who had not been of the digging party. The effect in the curative action was such as to make all exercise or exertion impossible & complete rest was ordered by the A.D.M.S. Men who appeared unaffected went about helping their comrades or doing their ordinary work & would collapse suddenly & unaccountably. Even several days later when many appeared to have recovered, the slightest exercise caused a set-back. Between 20° & 25° T.O.R. were also affected (of whom 5 S.D.S.E.) but not suffering from gas poison.	
		3.0 a.	A party of 5 Officers & 150 O.R. to CRUCIFIX CORNER W.H.A. (Prior S.D.S.E.) for 12 hours carrying duties, taking rifle ammunition up to Battn. in front line.	
		9.5?	CAPT. R.G. NEWMAN, CAPT. C.C. DAVIES, Lt. J.R. BLAKE & Lt. A. PLAISTOWE Evacuated attached to b.b. Bn. & in addition Capt. A. Coy Commanders to place their heavy casualties of the week. + 2nd Lts. W.O.H. WILLIAMS, B.H. TULLIDGE, J.C. WICKHAM + S.H. WILKES + A.Peterson Cruickshanks.	

INTELLIGENCE SUMMARY. / 8th BATTN. THE WORCESTERSHIRE REGT.

(Erase heading not required.)

Place	Date	Hour	Summary of Events and Information	Remarks and references to Appendices
	JULY			
BOUZINCOURT	26	3.30pm	Battalion moved by Motor Transport to FRANSU (France [Sm.] 11 1:100,000 B5) 3 miles N.N.W.	
FRANSU			of DOMART, returning into X Corps from II. Here the men were in billets for 4 days before	
HOUDENCOURT	30	10am	being moved into open bivouacs at HOUDENCOURT 1½ miles East of FRANSU. Small numbers	
			continued to be evacuated to Hospital daily from sundry minor affections. A few	
	30.		prisoners of war well. Draft of 75 O.R., including 10 returned from Hospital.	
	31.		STRENGTH Officers 29 Other ranks 778	
			(fighting)	
			CASUALTIES. Killed in action Officers 1 O.R. 6	
			Died of wounds " nil " nil	
			Died of gas poison " nil " 2	
			Wounded " 1 " 40	
			Suffering from gas (to Hospital) " 3 " 113	
			Sick " "	
			Missing nil nil	
			Prisoners of war nil nil	
			31.7.16	
			Walter K. Clarke Ltr.	
			Comg 1/8 Bn The Worcestershire Regt	

INTELLIGENCE SUMMARY
1/8th BATTN. THE WORCESTERSHIRE REGT.

Place	Date	Hour	Summary of Events and Information	Remarks and references to Appendices
HOUDENCOURT	1916			
FRANSU	Aug 1		The Bn. formed up at station de HOUDENCOURT. Between 40 and 50 O.R. suffering from gas poisoning were unrelated to hospital while the Bn. was stationed here. The remainder of the gassed men were unfit for any exertion, and as they did not improve they were sent to the Guards' 3rd or 2nd Battalions depot of reinforcements.	
CAYEUX	Aug 7 Aug 16		The Bn. was transport and personnel marched to Lieut. HAWTREY remaining with 144 Brigade. was consigned to No 5 throughout camps near CAYEUX. Every effort was made to get the men fit, but it was found that any great men who took violent exercise such as Physical Training, Drill + Route march, the majority still showed unmistakable signs of gas poisoning – shortened friend, irregular action of heart, general debility etc. Thus before sent home most means to return the 48 Division.	
BOUZINCOURT	Aug 21		The Bn. entrained at S.VALERY sur SOMME, 5 miles N.E. of CAYEUX to the Div. railhead at ACHEUX, which was reached in the evening. Thence a march was made to the country W. of BOUZINCOURT (57D v.12a) where the Bn. bivouacked for the night. The unfit men were conveyed on vehicles of both halfs of the journey. Draft of 6 N.C.O.R joined the Bn.	
AVELUY	Aug 22		Headquarters and 3 fit men of the Bn. proceeded to CRUCIFIX CORNER, AVELUY,	

INTELLIGENCE SUMMARY
8th BATTN. THE WORCESTERSHIRE REGT.

(Erase heading not required.)

Place	Date	Hour	Summary of Events and Information	Remarks and references to Appendices
AVELUY	14th		FRANCE 57D.W.&C. relieve outposts near BENIFAY, the On. relieving 11th/7th Bn Royal Warwickshire Regt. 'C' coy. were in support to the 1/4th Bn GLOUCESTER-SHIRE and 'D'coy. with the 'B' Bn. of the same regt. the remaining two coys remained at CRUCIFIX CORNER and Battln working parties to railway went on. 'C' coy. occupied dugouts and shell cave original front line in front of and to the W. of RIDDLE WOOD and 'D' coy. was in the original BERNAM fort that is E (FINME 57D SE X 2.d.) – Casualties while engaged in these parties – One wounded.	
	15		In the relief 4 O.R. of 9th Royal [illeg.] Cmd [illeg.] returned to CRUCIFIX CORNER in default of joining the 4th on arrival at CAMP. Remained the same with the 5th Brigade Pioneers 2 Lt L.R. TURNER and 352 O.R. left for duty	
	16		The Bn left CRUCIFIX CORNER and proceeded to BOUZINCOURT WOOD (57D W4)	
BOUZINCOURT	26.7		Bn L.R. to RUBEMPVILLE (57D.O.P.1). It was left hand company in the trenches N.E. of AUCHONVILLERS (MAPS 57D Q4 & 9.4), the 2/4th R.F. being on the left and 11/7th Bn WORCESTERSHIRE

INTELLIGENCE SUMMARY.

1/8th BATTN. THE WORCESTERSHIRE REGT.

(Erase heading not required.)

Summaries are contained in F.S. Regs., Part II. and the Staff Manual respectively. Title pages will be prepared in manuscript.

Place	Date	Hour	Summary of Events and Information	Remarks and references to Appendices
AUTHUILLE TRENCHES	1916		Bn. on Brigade in left sector, with Bn. Commanded HdQrs at MAILLY MAILLET. Btn. went up to the trenches that night, & was relieved the next day at 8 p.m. by 1/7 Worc'rs (relief was carried out successfully without incident) & came back into Brigade reserve. The total casualties at 30 minutes 2nd were 11 O.R. wounded, of B ; 14 Officers and 470 O.R. Returns.	

G.A. Gee Pask
Lieut.-Colonel,
Commanding 1/8th Bn. The Worcestershire Regiment

WAR DIARY
INTELLIGENCE SUMMARY

1/8th BATTN. THE WORCESTERSHIRE REGT.

Place	Date	Hour	Summary of Events and Information	Remarks and references to Appendices
AUCHONVILLERS TRENCHES	Sept 1		During the remainder of the tour the weather continued to be bad, and the trenches especially those held by the left coy (whose front line was only 4 feet deep in parts), was continually being filled in by minenwerfer fire from the N.W. corner of BEAUMONT HAMEL) soon became very wet. Hostile artillery was also active nightly on our return dumps, but did no damage.	
	2			
	3	2.00	About 10.30 P.M. the enemy started to bombard the villages and battery positions in rear of our line with gas shells. A few also fell on the left of our front but did no harm. This shelling lasted till 4 A.M. on the 3rd. At dawn on the 3rd an attack was launched against the	
		5.10 A.M.	front three lines of German trenches, on either side of the River ANCRE; the 39th attached on a front of 4 Coys north of the river, and the 49th Divn on a similar front south of the river. Both attacks at first partially succeeded, but by 9.15 A.M. we were driven back to our original front line. During the attack our line received some attention, about on the right coy line being trenched in 8 the casualties (4) buried. On the night 3rd-4th 140 were discharged from the 7 Worc.	
	4		Regt's front on our immediate right, apparently very successfully.	
	5	3 P.M.	The Bn was relieved by 1st BUCKS Bn & marched to MAILLY MAILLET, whence motor buses took us	G. West
		6 P.M.	to hutments at BUS, the men's feet being in a bad condition owing to the weather conditions.	

Army Form C. 2118.

WAR DIARY
or
INTELLIGENCE SUMMARY.
(Erase heading not required.)

1/8th BATTN. THE WORCESTERSHIRE REGT

Instructions regarding War Diaries and Intelligence Summaries are contained in F. S. Regs., Part II. and the Staff Manual respectively. Title pages will be prepared in manuscript.

Place	Date	Hour	Summary of Events and Information	Remarks and references to Appendices
Hd.Qs. BUS.	6-8th		3rd Corps reserve to 5 Corps (8th) the G.O.C. inspected the Bn. (10th) 2/Lieut H.H. MILWARD (3rd Bn Worc Regt. attached) proceeded to ENGLAND upon M.G. School GRANTHAM. (12th) Lieut-Col. W.K. PEAKE was transferred to ENGLAND (sick)	
	13th	3.15 PM	The Bn moved to huts at AMPLIER. GLOUC. Regt. As the huts at AMPLIER were not considered habitable the Bn moved the same	
		4 PM	night to huts at AUTHIEULLE.	
	14th to 18th		While Bn training was carried out in musketry (improvised ranges being closed land) Gas warfare bayonet fighting (14th) 1 Off & 4 2 3 O.R. (wounded (Gassed) were evacuated to no.5 Consolescent Camp; they were formed into 2 Coys under Capts. BATE & DAVIES with 3 other officers, who under the orders of the O.C. Camp were to help to get these men fit again by gradual training. Eventually they are to be drafted to Bns. from the Base when they are again fit for duty.	
	19th	9.5 AM	Bn moved to OUTREBOIS the the Bn training was continued to the drafts arrived greatly leaving much keenness att Bde Hd.Qts. Inspection at BOISBERGUES (Snap-shooting) 5 & 6 places were reserved. Major L. KERWOOD	
	24th		relinquished command on being on aid on sick leave in command to 13th Bn CHESHIRE Regt & Major S.H. CLARK assumed command. Capt H.T. CLARKE rejoined from 46 I.B.D. ROUEN.	
	25th 26th	2 PM	Bn (less 2 Coys) moved to DOMESMONT, B 2 Coys A&C to EPECAMPS. (29th) MOVED TO OUTREBOIS	
	30th	9.45 AM	The Bn (less 1 Coy) moved to BEAUDICOURT. Staff B, D OPPY. He Bn being engaged at Corps FIGHTING STRENGTH 22 Officers 6130 O.R. CASUALTIES: 2 did of wounds, 8 wounded, 4 23 wounded (gassed)	

J.W. Clark Major
Commanding 8th Bn. The Worcestershire Regiment.

Army Form C. 2118.

WAR DIARY
or
INTELLIGENCE SUMMARY

(Erase heading not required.)

8th BATTN. THE WORCESTERSHIRE REGT.

Place	Date	Hour	Summary of Events and Information	Remarks and references to Appendices
BEAUCOURT	1916 Oct 1st	10.15 AM	The Bn. marched to HONNECOURT, only 2 hrs notice of the move was given.	
HONNECOURT	2nd		2nd Lieuts A.R.WATSON and R.N. HORSLEY, 7 Res. Bn. the Worc Regt reported for duty	
	3rd		A second draft of 70 O.R. under 2 Lt F. Wor. Yeomanry making a total of 150 O.R. Yeomanry happy, at this move, were of good physique and had had 2 years training as Cavalry, but are now only a fortnight as infantry.	
	4th		Bad weather stopped all training	
	5th			
	6th		Training on trenches carried out - one of the new shafts all blown in by bombs. Brigadier General NICHOLSON commanding 144 Inf Bde. inspected the Yeomanry drafts - training other shell and rifle bomb attack work carried out	
	7th		Battalion 32 less 2/Lt Attack one wound out.	
	8th		A & C Coys moved to the Fme de la HAIE, where the trenches employed gave	
	9th		Bn. (less A and C coys) moved to WARLINCOURT (FRANCE 57D c50)	
WARLINCOURT	10th		Training continued - more drafts Hour arms now hob back.	
	11th			
	12th		Lieut (QMr) H.A. CARR, D.S.O. the Worcestershire Regt assumed command, Major S.H. Fisk vacated the duties "Q.M." Bn. claiming officer -	

Army Form C. 2118.

WAR DIARY
or
INTELLIGENCE SUMMARY
(Erase heading not required.)

8th BATTN. THE WORCESTERSHIRE REGT.

Instructions regarding War Diaries and Intelligence Summaries are contained in F. S. Regs., Part II. and the Staff Manual respectively. Title Pages will be prepared in manuscript.

Place	Date	Hour	Summary of Events and Information	Remarks and references to Appendices
SOUASTRE		1.95 p.m.	The Bn. less A & C companies marched to billets in SOUASTRE (S.7.D. d. 2.)	
			B and C coys were attached at the Forme de la HAIE by 2 coys 4th Gloucestershire and rejoined the battalion	
TRENCHES			March: 8th Bn. moved to relieve 1/6 HEBUTERNE facing ROSSIGNOL PARK being relieved the 6th Gloucestershire Regt in the trenches. Day was quiet. C coy in support, and A coy in reserve in the KEEP front line being left front, B Coy Gloucestershire Regt were on our left, and the 7th Bn. E. HEBUTERNE the 6th (7th Div) on our right. The Bn held lines from N10 b 27 (refers Regt (7th Div)) — The relief was complete by 12 noon without casualties	
HEBUTERNE			Quiet day - We had a few small outpost line. During the night (17th-18th) our patrols encountered no enemy. The Germans were noticed working and were heard to be very busy completing their parapets and was encountered	
			In and out of 10 am on one in 6 or HEBUTERNE - Our patrols moving our and were fired by Lewis Gun fire. Officers of the 4th N.O.Y.L.T. reconnoitred the trenches	
	19. 3.11.		The Bn was relieved by the 4 Bn N.O.Y.L.T. Wrote my relief to SOUASTRE. Bn. marched to SOUASTRE had wounds and 2 wounded (self from shell fire)	

2449 Wt. W14957/M90 759,000 1/16 J.B.C. & A. Forms/C.2118/12.

INTELLIGENCE SUMMARY
WAR DIARY
or
INTELLIGENCE SUMMARY

(Erase heading not required.)

Army Form C. 2118.

1/8th BATTN. THE WORCESTERSHIRE REGT.

Instructions regarding War Diaries and Intelligence Summaries are contained in F. S. Regs., Part II. and the Staff Manual respectively. Title Pages will be prepared in manuscript.

Place	Date	Hour	Summary of Events and Information	Remarks and references to Appendices
SOUASTRE	20		2/Lieuts R.N. PITTARD and J.T. HILL (1st Reserve Bn Worc. Regt) reported for duty —	
		9.15 AM	Proceeded to BEAUMONT and were present in billets by 1.15 P.M. (LENS II E.4)	
BEAUMONT	21st		Day occupied in various inspections and general cleaning up —	
	22nd	9.30 AM	Sword Drills, followed by an Inspection by the Commanding Officer. The afternoon was occupied by Inter-platoon football matches.	
	23rd		The Bn. practised the attack from trenches which was represented by flags. Two companies in two waves had as their objective first line of enemy trenches, and the remaining two companies also in two waves the second line of enemy trenches.	
	24th		Bad weather stopped training, men were employed in adjusting their private kits for march into the Gas alert "position.	
	25		The Bn. moved in motor busses to BRESLE. The embussing wheel took place at IVERGNY was made very slow & confused owing to the fact that the Frenchmen in charge failed to understand what orders their Officers had given them.	

Army Form C. 2118.

INTELLIGENCE SUMMARY

WAR DIARY
or
INTELLIGENCE SUMMARY

(Erase heading not required.)

8th BATTN. THE WORCESTERSHIRE REGT.

Instructions regarding War Diaries and Intelligence Summaries are contained in F. S. Regs., Part II. and the Staff Manual respectively. Title Pages will be prepared in manuscript.

Place	Date	Hour	Summary of Events and Information	Remarks and references to Appendices
BRESLE	25		The Bn. occupied a camp at BRESLE which owing to the wet weather was most uncomfortable in many ways	
	26		Having now pretty settled in we had the bad weather	
	27		Rain fell again. The Commanding Officer and mounted officers reconnoitred the nature of the country to BRENTIN-QUEUTZ, MARTINSWICH and LESARS.	
	28		Billets at BACHEUX were allotted to the Bn.	
			The band played throughout the morning. In the afternoon a match between A & B Coys and C & D Coys took place, in which the former were beaten by 8 goals to 1.	
	29		The mounted officers reconnoitred the billets round LE SARS in the morning. A party of Officers & N.C.Os. proceeded on foot to the CONTALMAISON and from there the party proceeded & arrived at LE SARS. Shortly after their arrival very heavy snow fell in the afternoon and made the roads very bad.	
	30	AM	The Bn. marched (via MILLENCOURT) to ALBERT and were placed in billets.	

ALLAN
Commanding 8/Worc Regt

CONFIDENTIAL

WAR DIARY Sept 20
of
1ST WORCESTER REGT

From 1st Oct 1914 Nov 1914

(Vol X)

1914
#
20.Z

INTELLIGENCE SUMMARY

(Erase heading not required.)

8th BATTN. THE WORCESTERSHIRE REGT.

Place	Date 1916	Hour	Summary of Events and Information	Remarks and references to Appendices
ALBERT (W.28)	Nov 1	12.30 P.M.	x 16 b d. The Bn moved to CONTALMAISON which was reached at about 3 P.M. The men were partly in old dugouts and partly in shelters hastily scraped out of the side of the road. No hut of the latter had fallen in on account of the wind. No waterproof sheets were pitched at about 6 P.M. and occupied forthwith by C.O.D. Coy + amies.	Map France 57 D
CONTALMAISON (X16.d)	2	3 P.M.	The Bn moved to Intermediate relieving the 8-10 Bn. The Gordon Highlanders, 15th Division. The Line held was in front of LE SARS and was approximately 650 yds in length. The right resting on the MARTINPUICH — WARLENCOURT-EAUCOURT road (M16087) and the left at M16a 39 — A Coy were right hut coy, B. left half. C in support in "The CUTTING" (M16 c 51) and D Coy in reserve in O.92 "(M17a3s) The relief was carried out with only one casualty and was complete by 10.30 P.M. The trenches were in a very bad state, unrevetted and without trench boards. A.A. communication trenches were impassable. The relief was carried out entirely across the open. The night was fairly quiet, LE SARS being intermittently shelled as well as our front and support lines. Our patrols went out and brought back useful information of the ground in front of us. That obtained by a patrol led by 2/Lieut S. HUGHES being especially valuable.	FRANCE 57c
	3		The day was fairly quiet, the usual shelling taking place. At night our patrols were again active and returned with fuller particulars of Romans Land.	do. do.

INTELLIGENCE SUMMARY

(Erase heading not required.)

/8th BATTN. THE WORCESTERSHIRE REGT.

Instructions regarding War Diaries and Intelligence Summaries are contained in F.S. Regs., Part II. and the Staff Manual respectively. Title Pages will be prepared in manuscript.

Place	Date	Hour	Summary of Events and Information	Remarks and references to Appendices
TRENCHES LE SARS (M16)	4 Nov 1916		Enemy artillery was more active and the whole Bn area was fairly heavily and continuously shelled. During the evening coys relieved "A" coy going into Reserve, "B" into Support, "C" left half, and "D" right half. Our patrols were again active but met none of the enemy.	Map. FRANCE.57c
	5.		During the morning the 50th Div on our right attacked the SOTTE de WARLENCOURT M.17.d.27. But as far as could be observed from our lines were incomplete successful. The retaliation for the barrage which preceded their attack was heavy, and all our area was very heavily shelled. At about 3 P.M. an order was received that a patrol was to go out and discover the position of the left flank of the 50th Division. Lieut. A. PLAISTOWE and Lieut. CRUMP went out, and though they were fired on by rifles and Machine Guns - in addition to having to go through the German barrage they returned safely with the valuable information that the 50th Division had their left hand post in the QUARRY M.17.c.07. Later on Lieut. SWALLOW was sent out to obtain the same information, as Mr PLAISTOWE took longer than his Company Commander had thought he would. He also returned with the same information, at about 6 P.M. orders from Brigade were received that a new trench was to be dug from M.16.b.24 to the QUARRY, to consolidate our new line - Later information was received that the relieving Bn ("B" Glouc. Regt) would do this. The Bn	do. do.

INTELLIGENCE SUMMARY

1/8th BATTN. THE WORCESTERSHIRE REGT.

(Erase heading not required.)

Instructions regarding War Diaries and Intelligence Summaries are contained in F.S. Regs., Part II. and the Staff Manual respectively. Title Pages will be prepared in manuscript.

Place	Date	Hour	Summary of Events and Information	Remarks and references to Appendices
LE SARS	Nov 5 1916 contd		was ordered to detail an officer to go out and tape the new track out with an R.E. Officer 2/Lieut W.H. GRIFFITHS while engaged on this was badly wounded in the back and legs. The work which was considerably delayed owing to the number of casualties which had to be evacuated, & owing to the heavy shelling, was completed by 11 P.M. Casualties during the day in the Trenches were 2/Lieut [illegible] 2/Lt W H GRIFFITHS wounded	MAP FRANCE 57 D
SCOTTS REDOUBT X.21.b	6"		The Bn reached SCOTTS REDOUBT at about 1 A.M. [X 21.b.] most of the men being tired out though all were in excellent spirits. Day was spent resting and cleaning up.	57 D
TRENCHES			2nd in Cmd Major Sam Gill and Walter was very cold. Baths were [illegible] to the Bn in the afternoon and at 3.15 P.M. Bn moved to trenches from MARTINPUICH and BAZENTIN LE PETIT. Bn Hqrs were at S.3.a.77½ STARFISH [S.2.c] B Coy was in SWANSEA LEFT and RIGHT and two in [S.2.a]	57 C
TRENCHES	8"		Bn was engaged in working parties carrying material & clearing MARTINPUICH and in clearing communication trenches between MARTINPUICH and LE SARS.	
	9"		The work was continued – Draft of 25 [illegible] for [illegible] to company.	

INTELLIGENCE SUMMARY

1/8th BATTN. THE WORCESTERSHIRE REGT.

Instructions regarding War Diaries and Intelligence Summaries are contained in F.S. Regs., Part II. and the Staff Manual respectively. Title Pages will be prepared in manuscript.

(Erase heading not required.)

Place	Date 1916	Hour	Summary of Events and Information	Remarks and references to Appendices
	Nov			MAP FRANCE 57D
	10	5 P.M.	Bn. was relieved by the 4 Bn. Ox & Bucks L.I. and marched back to tents billets at PEAKE WOOD Camp (X.22.d.59) RIGHT All coys were present in billets at 8.30 P.M.	
PEAKE WOOD X.22.d.	11		Men were employed in clearing up and making paths round camp etc. Most of the camp was composed of shelters roofed by bivouac sheets, the others being in tents.	
	12		Bde. Chap. parade – Working parties amounting to 200 men were found, and were busy making between MARTIN PUICH & BAZENTIN, making material for MARTIN PUICH, and making camps in BAZENTIN.	
	13		Parties amounting to 250 men found for number of Bn. handed for Pozières. Owing to this man dull. Small parties were found.	
	14		Working parties of 300 were found, work continued as for 12th.	
	15		Parties of 250 found. A & B Coys. made packed the attack from billets in the neighbourhood of the camp.	
	16		Same parties. C & D coys practised the attack.	
	17		Same parties. Very heavy rain fell all day.	
	18			
	19		Bn. moved into support in MARTIN PUICH, relieving the 2 Royal Bucks – 22nd of 50 Brigade. See account of general operations	

2449 Wt. W14957/M90 750,000 1/16 J.B.C. & A. Forms/C.2118/12.

INTELLIGENCE SUMMARY

or

(Erase heading not required.)

1/8th BATTN. THE WORCESTERSHIRE REGT.

Place	Date 1916	Hour	Summary of Events and Information	Remarks and references to Appendices
MARTINPUICH	NOV. 20	4.30 PM	The Bn moved to the trenches previously occupied in front of LE SARS, relieving 1/6th Glouc. Regt. "A" Coy in right front, "D" Coy left front, "B" support, and "C" reserve. The relief was complete by 10.45 P.M. with one casualty. The night was quiet apart from the enemy shelling. Our patrols under 2/Lts CLUTTERBUCK and POTTER brought back useful information but met no hostile patrols.	
	21	2 AM	Heavy shelling around LE SARS. A patrol B1 N.C.O. and 2 men of "D" Coy who went out at 2 A.M. (22nd) failed to return. Probably they lost direction completely owing to the thick fog. Two patrols under 2/Lieut POTTER searched in vain for them.	
	22		The day was quiet until about 4.30 P.M. when the enemy started to shell LE SARS, SUNKEN road and our communications very heavily, using a large number of "Tear" shells. This delayed the 4 Glouc Regt. in their way up to relieve us. At 11 P.M. the relief was complete, the bn being now handled in having only one casualty.	
MARTINPUICH	23	1 AM.	Bn billets present on left support bn Place MARTINPUICH, one Coy "C" in	

INTELLIGENCE SUMMARY

(Erase heading not required.)

of 8th BATTN. THE WORCESTERSHIRE REGT.

Instructions regarding War Diaries and Intelligence Summaries are contained in F.S. Regs., Part II. and the Staff Manual respectively. Title Pages will be prepared in manuscript.

Place	Date 1916	Hour	Summary of Events and Information	Remarks and references to Appendices
MARTINPUICH	Nov 23rd		26th Division "B" coy near Cat Trench (M33a19) "A" coy in MARTINPUICH (M33a19) & "D" coy in MARTINPUICH (M32b24) near the church.	Map FRANCE 57C
	24th		Bn formed working parties in village, salving material and clearing trenches. At 6 P.M. the Bn was relieved by the 6th Bn. Royal Warwickshire Regt & moved to SHELTER WOOD CAMP (X22.38) being present by 10.30 P.M.	57 D
SHELTER WOOD CAMP	25th 26th		The day was spent cleaning up. Working parties strength 150 were found, hutting & working at Div. (HQ grs.)	"
SCOTTS REDOUBT NTH CAMP	27th 28th		Bn moved to SCOTT'S REDOUBT NORTH (X24 b.94)	
			Bn. Same working parties were found. The remainder of the men were employed improving the camp. The G.O.C. 144th Inf Bde congratulated the effects RAYER & CLUTTERBUCK on their good patrol work, and the G.O.C 48th Div. also congratulated the Commanding Officer on the good work done by the Bn in the trenches. A wire was received stating that the following had been awarded the military medal 2737 P/Cpl Roughll, 20320 Pte Flack, 4895 Pte Batty, 4965 Pte Wood 18794 Pte Constable.	
	29th 30th		Same working parties. A.B.C. coys practised the attack. Some parties were found.	

Commanding 8th Bn. The Worcestershire Regiment.

H. G. Clarke
Major

Confidential

War Diary
of
1st Worcestershire Regiment

from 1st October 1916
to 31st December 1916

Army Form C.2118.

52

WAR DIARY
or
INTELLIGENCE SUMMARY

(Erase heading not required.)

1/6th Bn the Warwickshire Regt.

Place	Date 1916	Hour	Summary of Events and Information	Remarks and references to Appendices
Scotts Redoubt NORTH x 21.c.94	Dec 1st		Bn. supplied working parties of 2 offrs + 100 O.R. for work on CONTALMAISON - VILLA RD. 2/Lt. and 75 O.R. — carrying and unloading for 1st W. Coy. R.E. 1 offr + 500 for work at Div. H.Q. making water supply. Remainder of Bn. employed in improving camp.	WW
	2nd	2.45 p.m	Bn. moved to trenches previously occupied in front of LE SARS and relieved 1/6 Bn. R. Warwickshire Regt. D Coy right front, C Coy left front, A Coy support B Coy reserve. Relief completed by 7.45 pm with two casualties. Our patrols never got to N.E. CLUTTERBUCK J.T. IBBS and R.M. PITTARD (never got back useful information — no enemy encountered.	WW
LE SARS TRENCHES	3rd		During the day small enemy shelling round LE SARS. At night a considerable artillery strong fire according to scheme previously arranged up but enemy late but it is thought that our own shells were constantly bursting in SMALL WOOD (M10.c.93) The raiding party was unable to advance past the front edge of the wood and could not reach the enemy lines as enormous no. of our own shells also burst behind SCOTLAND TRENCH 25% 7 gun more shells also burst in "No MAN'S LAND" though this percentage on foremisen. The party returned with no casualties — Useful information was obtained. 2/Lt S.H. WILKES was in charge of the raiding party + 2/Lts W.H. REYNOLDS in charge of supporting platoon. Patrols under 2/Lts. N.E. CLUTTERBUCK + J.E. RAYER also went out and brought in useful information.	WW
	4th		Usual shelling round LE SARS, DESTREMONT FARM and 26th AVENUE. Aerial activity by enemy and ourselves. Work was carried out improving the trenches which were in a very bad condition. In the evening a continuation of relief was carried out - A Coy relieving D in right front + B Coy relieving C	WW

Report on Raid
1/3. WORCS.

The raid ~~party~~ on started as per scheme, but owing to the fact that our own shells were constantly bursting in small wood at M10 c.9.3 the raiding party was unable to advance past the front edge of this wood, and could not enter enemy line as arranged. Six a ~~section~~ ~~quantity of~~ shells also burst behind SCOTLAND TRENCH.

Information obtained: There appears to be no post in the small wood, which does not look as if it had ever been occupied. There also appears to be no German listening posts in front of SCOTLAND TR as reputed in Summary of Intelligence. —
There is a ruined house in the small

(Twenty five per cent of our own shells burst in NO MAN'S LAND, and half of this percentage on percussion in NO MAN'S LAND)

wood, which originally contained well over fifty trees. —

4/12/16.

J.P. Bate Capt
COVER.

STORES Required.

2 BANGALORE TORPEDOES.

16 CLUBS.

6 LONG PATTERN WIRE CUTTERS.

24 BOXES N°5 GRENADES.

24 ELECTRIC TORCHES.

2 6 ft. Ladders.

8 8 ft. LIGHT TRENCH BOARDS
   (for bridging)

400 YARDS TRACING TAPE.

20 GRENADE CARRIERS.

6 "T" Combs.

3.

COMPOSITION OF RAIDING PARTY.

"A"
o oo
oo
{ LEFT SIDE Corporal & 4 men.
2 rifles and bayonets with 6
bombs each. 2 bombers 12 bombs
each. Bomber bayonets & clubs.
           2 wirecutts

"B"
o oo
oo
oo
{ ADVANCE PARTY
Sgt and 6 men. 2 Rifles & bayonets
2 bombers with clubs & bayonets
2 carriers   "   "   "

"C"
8
oo
oo
oo
{ MAIN PARTY
2 Lt WILKES and 6. O.R.
6 bombers with 6 bombs each, also
6 "P" bombs, armed with clubs
and bayonets

"D"
o oo
oo
oo
{ EXIT GUARD.   1 officer and
1 N.C.O. and 5 men with
rifles and bayonets
12 Bombs (bombing men
[last]) 2 Lts ladders, to be dug
and tracing tape

oooo
PARADOS PARTY
1 N.C.O and 3 men to remain goating

Strength 2 OFFICERS.   kanados keeping
          25 O.R.   touch with
                       main party.

1 Platoon in outpost 30 yards
bright.

ORDERS.

1. Party will assemble at junction of track and LE SARS TK; NORTH. at 3ero – 12 R.

2. Party will leave assembly trench at zero – 1½, proceed along track and take up position boyning from enemy wire at zero – 15.

3. At zero time, barrage will start.
   Ce BANGALORE TORPEDO will be exploded in wire, and an entrance made.

4. "A" party (Left stop) with move to left and make a stop 20 yds from point of entry.

   "B" party (Advance party) will bomb down trench in direction of SUNKEN ROAD.

   "C" party (Main party) will keep in touch with advance party, and do as much damage as possible.

"D" party (Exit guard) will place ladders in trench, and prepare the way for a rapid exit.

5. If condition of trench is bad the raid will be carried out along the parados, using the 2 8ft bridges.

6. The party will not stay in the trench longer than necessary.

7. The support [station] will cross NO MANS LAND 35 yds behind raiding party, during raid it will be 30 yards from entry point. The officer in command of it will be responsible for keeping touch with exit guard.

Zerotime if possible
        9 AM on a foggy morning
If weather not suitable, start
4 AM.
                J.P.B....
2.8.16.   C.O.
                    1/8 WORCS.

SECRET

Headquarters
1/4 Infy Bde   30.XI.16

Ref:ce RAIDS

When this Bn was last in the line the enemy had various small posts out at night in front of BUTTE TRENCH about M 17 a 6 3.

I would propose to locate one or more of these posts exactly and to capture them at night by means of a party of 1 Officer + 20 O.R. who would move out from MAXWELL TRENCH and be supported by 1 Officer 10 OR + a LEWIS GUN.

For artillery support I would ask for a 2 minute rapid barrage on the point selected followed by a 10 minute slow box barrage.

I cannot give exact objective until this Bn returns to the line + I ascertain the present state of affairs.

F.M.Tomkinson
Lt Col Comdg
1/7 Worces Regt

SCHEME FOR RAID ON ENEMY LINE.

Ref. LE SARS trench map 9ᴬ
and sketch map herewith.

OBJECTS: 1. To kill Germans.
2. To take prisoners.
3. To obtain information.

IDEA. To enter GALLWITZ TR: at point where track leaving our line at M16A8580 cuts enemy front line at M10D1537; to proceed from that point to junction of enemy front line and SUNKEN ROAD and then to return. During time of occupation of enemy line, barrage to be kept by field guns in line from point M10C96 to left, ~~of communication trench~~ to M10C8590, thence along enemy ~~front line~~ to SUNKEN ROAD. Howitzers also employed if available, advice to be taken from ~~~~ ~~~~ ~~as follows.~~

~~Barrage in separate~~ following

144 Inf. Bde.   APP "C" 26

The attached Scheme for a Raid on the enemy's line during the next tour in the trenches is submitted for approval, please.

H. T. Clarke.
Major
Comdg 1/8 Worc. Regt.

28.XI.16.

Remarks
2 officers to accompany raiding party
~~Form~~
Scout for wirelers
Is there any wire in front of enemy trench.
Would there be Bangalore Torpedoes
3 men Barrage along front trench at point & then left & form pocket — & a exit & foot trench
Is there a machine gun here
Signal for exit to be put up — barrage on
Telephones, bad idea use a series of posts better to go along parados

Army Form 2118 53/

WAR DIARY or **INTELLIGENCE SUMMARY**
(Erase heading not required.)

1/8 Bn. the Warwickshire Regt.

Place	Date 1916	Hour	Summary of Events and Information	Remarks and references to Appendices
LE SARS TRENCHES	Dec 4th		C Coy in left front. Bn. at 11.30 p.m. Enemy was approached the left attempt of our left front Coy (M.16.a.55.95) The Huns allowed the enemy to come quite close then opened fire. One enemy at once turned round and ran Chased by our men for 150 yds. but without result. One man no casualties. 2/Lt. Patrols went out during the night and provided information was obtained. A.F. RAIKES and R.T. KEEN awarded the MILITARY CROSS for gallantry and devotion to duty on Nov 5th in LE SARS.	MM
	5th		Enemy actively mining LE SARS and outpost trenches. Work was carried out in front of the trenches. Patrols under 2/Lt. S.H. WILKES and C.N.H. FRANKLIN went out and returned safely.	MM
	6th		Fairly quiet during the day. Bn. relieved by 1/5 R. Warwickshire Regt. Relief completed at 8.30 p.m. Bn. returned to Battln at SCOTTS REDOUBT N. and 11.25 p.m. Detail casualties for the town 1 killed 11 wounded.	MM
SCOTTS R.DT. NORTH	7th		Bn. employed in cleaning out + refitting. 2/Lt. E.W. MITCHELL reported for duty from 7th res. Bn. – 280 reinforcements – survivors – from No 5 Camp.	MM
	8th		Bn. supplied working party of 2 offs + 45 or thereabouts to MARTINPUICH Rly. Bank. All other ranks (X.17.b.80) allotted to Bn. MANETZ WOOD compiled camps congratulating troops on work done in spite of very adverse weather conditions.	MM
	9th 10th		Bn. Cmd. Trying to get billets in MARTINPUICH and relieved the 1/5 R. WARWICKSHIRE REGT. A + D Coys in 26th AVE. C Coy in MARTIN PUICH + B Coy in VILLA CAMP. Relief completed at 11.35 p.m.	MM MM

2449 Wt. W14957/M90. 750,000 1/16 J.B.C. & A. Forms/C.2118/12.

Army Form C. 2118.

54

1/3/13 th Worcestershire Regt.

WAR DIARY
or
INTELLIGENCE SUMMARY

(Erase heading not required.)

Instructions regarding War Diaries and Intelligence Summaries are contained in F.S. Regs., Part II. and the Staff Manual respectively. Title Pages will be prepared in manuscript.

Place	Date 1916	Hour	Summary of Events and Information	Remarks and references to Appendices
MARTINPUICH	11th		Bn supplied small working parties during the day for R.E. At night Bn provided carrying parties for wiring material, bombs & water to front line trenches. Two patrols went out through pts 1/14 & 1/14 N.E. GLOUCESTERSHIRE Regt. Reconnoitred the frontier M166, 2.90th N.E. CLUTTERBUCK + J.E. RYDER were in command respectively. 2nd Lt. N.E. CLUTTERBUCK's patrol came under heavy fire and suffered one casualty. Both patrols returned with useful information etc.	
	12th		Bn supplied working parties during the day collecting Germans bombs + R.E. material in MARTINPUICH. During the night working parties as before.	
LE SARS TRENCHES	13th		Bn relieved 1/4 GLOUCESTERSHIRE Regt. in the trenches previously occupied in front of LE SARS. Bay left front - C coy right front - D coy support + A coy reserve. Relief complete at 10.30 pm. Artillery annoying B + D coys. 5 H. WILKES 1 N.C.O + 6 men left SCOTLAND TR. at 11.45 pm at point M.16.a. 55.95 + proceeded north for 150 yards, they then turned half left + remained halted in course of exploration scanning ground in that direction + encountered enemy post behind some sandbag hurricane lamp. The patrol halted + fired three volts rifle fire and succeeded in killing three Germans for certain + presumably obtained more artillery honours. The patrol then returned to the trenches.	
	14th		Much enemy shelling of ourselves, LE SARS and support trenches. Bn. offrs for in SCOTLAND TRENCH suffered and hit from a 5.9. One man being killed + one wounded. This more or [unclear]

Army Form C. 2118.
55

1/5 Bath Hertfordshire Regt.

WAR DIARY
or
INTELLIGENCE SUMMARY
(Erase heading not required.)

Place	Date 1916	Hour	Summary of Events and Information	Remarks and references to Appendices
LE SARS TRENCHES	15		Bn relieved by the 12th H.L.I. Relief complete by 11.20 p.m. Bn proceeded to SCOTT'S REDOUBT CAMP N. and were relieved. Officers present in trenches were 2nd Lt S.W. WILKES and E.G. POTTER. Bn - 1.30 am 2nd Lts S.W. WILKES and E.G. POTTER remained in the trenches during attack of the returning Bn and rejoined the Bn at SCOTT'S REDOUBT CAMP at 2.30 p.m. Total casualties for the tour - 8 killed and 12 wounded - 8 O.R.'s, 2 and 4 wounded.	m
MAMETZ WOOD CAMP	16		Bn moved from SCOTT'S REDOUBT CAMP N. to MAMETZ WOOD CAMP (X 23 c 63) under orders of G.O.C. in Camp to a new site constructed - Guard attending in getting Camping. Bn arrived at Camp at 11.30 p.m.	m
	17th		Bn reorganized. Reinforcements - 1 Off + 30 O.R.'s for work and another 2 Officers Bn R.E. 114 + 20 O.R.'s for work with 2/Lt S.H. BRADLEY R.E. - 111 + 60 O.R.'s for work with 2/Lt HARVEY R.E. 2/Lts. N.F. CLUTTERBUCK and S.H. WILKES (in command) received and joined the Bn. Total officers of Bn in ALBERT. Remainder of Bn worked in improving Camp.	m
	18th		Arthur Saither Bn. The Bn employed by Oliver employer in improving camp Bn G.O.C. Bde. allotted entire leave 6.30 on for food. Work on defence outside camp. Work on defence.	m
	19		Work as before.	m
	20		Work on defences. During the night the camp was shelled at 7.15 am 3 am + 5.30 am. Bazintin (sharp) m

WAR DIARY
or
INTELLIGENCE SUMMARY

(Erase heading not required.)

Army Form C. 2118.

1/8 Bn. 1/8 Bn Worcestershire Rgt.

Place	Date 1916	Hour	Summary of Events and Information	Remarks and references to Appendices
MAMETZ WOOD CAMP	20th		Nil	
	21st		Work as before	
	22nd		Work as before. Bn. less 100 men in ALBERT around FRICOURT CAMP (reserves)	
	23rd		Bn. paraded in billets at 4 pm	
			Work as before. Capt. J.M. LANG, R.A.M.C. reported for duty.	
	24th		Work as before. Training curtain cancelled except for 2/Lt + 75 men for working parties.	
	25th		Remainder of Bn. at disposal of O.C. Coys for inspections	
	26th		Work as before	
	27th		Work as before. Div. Band played in Camp. during afternoon. 2/Lt. N.E. CLOTTERBUCK + 5 N.C.Os + 100 men marched to ALBERT where attached to 2nd/5th BH TULLIDGE & A.R. SOMERSET	
	28th		Work as before	
	29th		Work as before	
	30th	9 am	Bn. marched to BAISIEUX in the following order I.C.S. Brunna, A.D.B.C. Platoons at 100 pace interval. Bn. placed in billets 5:45 pm.	
BAISIEUX	31st		Coys at disposal of Coy. Commanders for foot + rifle inspections. Church parade at 11 am.	

Mair
Lieut.-Colonel,
Commanding 1/8th Bn. The Worcestershire Regiment.

Certificate
Want of [?]
Pat to to Mecheoles [?]

Army Form

WAR DIARY or INTELLIGENCE SUMMARY

(Erase heading not required.)

1/8th Bn. The Worcestershire Regt.

Instructions regarding War Diaries and Intelligence Summaries are contained in F.S. Regs., Part II. and the Staff Manual respectively. Title Pages will be prepared in manuscript.

Place	Date	Hour	Summary of Events and Information	Remarks and references to Appendices
BAISIEUX	Jan 1		Training in the morning. Christmas celebrated in the afternoon; 25th Dec being unsuitable.	
	2		Training as per training scheme.	
	3		do do Capt. C.C. DAVIES left Bn. for extra regimental employ.	
	4		do do	
	5		do do	
	6		Training as per Scheme in the morning. In the afternoon Bn. inspected by Lt.Gen. Sir W.P. PULTENEY K.C.B. K.C.M.G. D.S.O. who wished the men to train their hardest and keep fit for the coming offensive.	
	7	2 am.	The Bn. have received orders to move to No. 5 Training area for completing the journey ST SACVEUR (5 m. N.N.W. AMIENS) where it stays the night, completing the journey the following day. Church parade was held in the morning.	
	8		Training as in Training Scheme – At 5.15 am. the Bn. arrived at HEILLY (AMIENS 17 16 – M9 07' – 2° 32') where it entrained, detraining at PONT REMY (5 m. S.E. B ABBEVILLE) where it marched to DOUDELAINVILLE (ABBEVILLE 14 - 50 05' – 1 46'). Very bad weather during the march. Bn. transport unfortunately on lorry which occupied 1½ hours baggage by road and 2 lorries at each end of the railway journey for conveying up troops &c from the railway station. Bn. established itself in DOUDELAINVILLE & transport at WARCHEVILLE about 1 m. N.W. Bn. present in billets at 6.30 p.m.	
DOUDELAIN- VILLE	10		Coys at disposal of Coy. commanders for inspections. D Coy moved to billets in WARCHE- VILLE – accommodation insufficient at DOUDELAINVILLE.	
	11		Training as per Training Scheme	
	12		do do	

WAR DIARY / INTELLIGENCE SUMMARY

Army Form C. 2118.

1/8 Worcestershire Regt.

Place	Date	Hour	Summary of Events and Information	Remarks and references to Appendices
BOUZINCOURT	Jan. 13		Training as per Training Scheme	
	14		Voluntary service	
	15		Training as per Training Scheme	
	16		Bn. inspected by Brig. Gen. G.H. NICHOLSON C.B., in arms (according to formation laid down in Bde. Training Orders) at 11 a.m.	
	17		Heavy fall of snow during night, continuous during day. Training as per Training Scheme	
	18		Coys. practised training in the attack	
	19		do do	
	20		do do	
	21		Voluntary service	
	22		Bn. paraded in fighting order and marched to HALLENCOURT for Bde. exercise. Returned at 7 p.m.	
	23		do do do 6 p.m.	
	24		Coys. at disposal of Coy. commanders for inspections etc. Rifles inspected by Armourer Sgt. ACD. 1/2 Officers + 180 OR. attended concert given by Miss LENA ASHWELL's Party.	
	25		Training as per Training Scheme	
	26		do do	
	27		do do	
	28		Bn. paraded in Column of Route at 3.45 a.m. and marched to OISEMONT (DISPRE 16 49.657' - 1.047') and entrained. Left OISEMONT at 7.30 a.m. and detrained at WARFUSÉE (AMIENS 57½ 9° E8½ - 9°35') at 2 p.m. Bn. then marched to CERISY (AMIENS 57½ 17-49 9°54'- 9°32') Billeted in billets 3.30 p.m.	
	29		Coy. training	
	30		do do	
	31		do do do + a lecture which started our 15th gill conference	

H.W. Carr Lieut. Colonel,
Commanding 1/8 Bn. The Worcestershire Regt.

WAR DIARY
or
INTELLIGENCE SUMMARY
(Erase heading not required.)

Army Form C. 2118.

1/8th Bn. The Worcestershire Regt

Place	Date 1917	Hour	Summary of Events and Information	Remarks and references to Appendices
Sophie French Trench HERBECOURT	Feb 1		Battⁿ moved to Sophie Trench 1 mile West of HERBECOURT (map sheet AMIENS 17 49°55' - 2°51') and relieved 1/5th Battⁿ R Warwick Regt. Relief complete 1.30 p.m. Battⁿ accommodated in trenches with dugouts for all ranks. Hard frost. "C" Coy. 2 Off^s + 100 OR worked at detonating bombs under Div. Bomb. O/^r	War
	2		Coys. worked improving trenches & dugouts. "D" Coy furnishing 1 off + 100 OR detonating bombs	4 pm
	3		Improvement of trenches continued	6 am
	4		Voluntary service held in trenches	4 pm
	5		Inspections & improvements continued	4 pm
	6		do	4 pm
FRONT LINE	7		Battⁿ relieved 1/4th Gloucestershire Regt in front line trenches. "A" Coy Reserve "B" Coy left front "D" Coy right front. "C" Coy working Coy. Relief complete at 9 pm with no casualties. Line held O.1 c. 95.15 to O.1 b 15.95 on front of LA MAISONNETTE. Battⁿ on right 1/7 "R" WARWICKS Battⁿ on left 1/7 "R" WORCS REGT. Men worked in trenches which were in good condition owing to continued hard frost. Very quiet.	4 pm
	8		Again very quiet during day. Battⁿ relieved by 1/4th Batt. Dev. Bucks L.I. Relief complete at 9.30 p.m. two slight casualties. Battⁿ proceed in Camp 50 ECLUSIER at midnight	4 pm
ECLUSIER	9		Battⁿ employed cleaning up Camp which was very dirty. Church Parade service by Rev. J.B. FRITH. Battⁿ supplied working party 1 off 106 OR for work at HERBECOURT also 1 off 2 Platoons on work at BH' NQ. Capt. JONES left Batt to return to medical duties. Remainder carried on Company training.	4 pm
	10			
	11			4 pm
	12		Some working parties as on 11 inst. Remainder carried on Company training.	6 am
	13		As on 12 inst.	4 pm

Army Form C. 2118.

WAR DIARY or INTELLIGENCE SUMMARY

(Erase heading not required.)

Army Form C. 2118.

8th Bn. The Worcestershire Regt.

Place	Date 1917	Hour	Summary of Events and Information	Remarks and references to Appendices
ECLUSIER	Feb 14		Some working parties. Batt" moved to Camp s.6. CAPPY at 4.30 pm. The drums of the 2nd Batt" played us into Camp. The second Batt" lying at SUZANNE	
CAPPY	15		Men not employed on Camp paraded for inspection & Company training	
	16	5am	Enemy aeroplane overhead dropping bombs about 50 but without damage. Divisional area exploding ammn dump No 1 the SOMME. Batt" supplies working parties & attended Baths at ECLUSIER. Company Commanders reconnoitred Support line	
HERBECOURT	17	2 pm	Batt" moved into Bde Reserve B & C Coys in "Sophia" A Coy HERBECOURT. D Coy billeted FLAUCOURT Batt" relieved 1/5 "Gloucestershire Regt" A B	
	18		A B & C Coys worked improving trenches, material from Div Dump. D Coy parade 6 pm work on Coy Gun reconnoitred left Brigade line. Companies employed on continued improvement of trenches	[Front area on A]
	19	4.30 am	up to 2 pm. 6 pm 450 OR & Offrs employed working on forward area	
	20	2 pm	Working parties employed previous evening returned 2 am	
		6 pm	Working parties again nature but cancelled at the desire of the Brinkly. Offr own & to relieve next day	
FRONT LINE	21	4 pm	Batt" moved to front trenches to relieve the 1/4th Gloucestershire Regt. C Coy left front. D Coy centre A Coy held front. D Coy in Reserve in DESIRE Trench in H 36 c. Relief very difficult, trenches almost impassable owing to mud after thaw. Many O.R. Slooters got stuck & were carried on stretchers Relief completed 4 am 22 . Batt" HQ left g.7. WORKS	
	22		Day broke very misty, therefore observation bad. Enemy in trench Jst. NoSaB, to trench. Good track was shells from SUNKEN ROAD to Adv Batt" HQ. m night g. R.WARWICKS	
	23		All trenches were in spite of efforts made to clear them. Capt. KINNMYLNE & 2nd LT BOMFORD rejoined from England. In consequence of the communication trench be kept up over the top a snipping therefore became active. Casualties for past 24 hours. 1 killed 7 wounded (6 by snipers)	

WAR DIARY or INTELLIGENCE SUMMARY

(Erase heading not required.)

Army Form C. 2118.

1/8th Bn. The Worcestershire Regt

Place	Date 1917	Hour	Summary of Events and Information	Remarks and references to Appendices
FRONT LINE	Feb 23	7.30	Reliefs Coy relieved Centre Coy & platoon reliefs carried out by Right & Left Coys.	nil
		7pm	Heavy bombardment warthead away to our right which quickly spread up to us & beyond. The S.O.S. was sent up in two places on the right & once on the left. The enemy did not come out of their trenches on our front. Our centre Company relief got caught in the barrage & suffered casualties 7 Coy 5 killed 7 wounded. The Lewis Gunner man was got out of the front line after personal efforts & reached Coy H.Q.	
"	24	5.50 am	Heavy bombardment on our Brigade front – our artillery replied. This continued until 6.30 am. Estimated casualties 1 killed 6 wounded. The remainder of the day quiet except for a few shells over whole area & "Gunsounders" on right of centre Coy. Total Casualties 15 Killed, 33 Wounded, 1 Died of Wounds	
	25		Day quiet. Battn relieved by 7th Ox & Bucks L.I. Relief conducted over busk road Rack. Relief completed 10.15pm	
HERBECOURT		12.15 am 26th	Battn in billets D + B Sectne 'A' HERBECOURT 'C' FLAUCOURT.	
CAPPY	26	2pm	Battn moved by platoons to Camp S6 CAPPY taking over from BUCKS BATT. 'C' Coy from FLAUCOURT arrived 8 pm.	nil
"	27		Working Parties 140 O.R. + 300 O.R. pervious 3 p.m.	nil
"	28		Working Party 300 returned 2 am & again paraded 3.30 pm	nil

J.H. Carr
Lieut-Colonel
Commanding 1/8th Bn. The Worcestershire Regiment

Confidential

1/8th Bn Worcestershire Regiment

WAR DIARY FOR MARCH 1917.

VOLUME 24.

Army Form C. 2118.

WAR DIARY
or
INTELLIGENCE SUMMARY.
(Erase heading not required.)

Instructions regarding War Diaries and Intelligence Summaries are contained in F. S. Regs., Part II. and the Staff Manual respectively. Title pages will be prepared in manuscript.

Place	Date	Hour	Summary of Events and Information	Remarks and references to Appendices

Instructions regarding War Diaries and Intelligence Summaries are contained in F. S. Regs., Part II. and the Staff Manual respectively. Title pages will be prepared in manuscript.

WAR DIARY
or
INTELLIGENCE SUMMARY.
(Erase heading not required.)

Army Form C. 2118.

Place	Date	Hour	Summary of Events and Information	Remarks and references to Appendices
TRENCHES S of BIACHES	Mar 1917		Coys continued trench improvement	
	16	7 pm	[illegible] sent for 145th Bde, 2 Coys 5th Glos & 2 Coys 1/4th Bn. Bucks L.I. who were to attack LA MAISONNETTE. [illegible] 2.30 am. B Coy 8th Worcs acted as Reserve to the attack.	HYC
	17	2.30 am	Attack successful reaching 2nd line without much trouble & finding enemy had evacuated from their line & fallen back East of the SOMME. The 1st Division on the right & the 143 Bde on left operated in conjunction. B Coy under Capt [illegible] on the [illegible] took part in the attack & materially assisted 5th Glos & captured & consolidated part of the enemy trenches. A Coy followed up & stayed in the original 1st & 2nd	HYC
	18		lines of the [illegible] getting in touch with 6th Glos on right & 5th Glos on left. Thus about 8 am on 18th inst. As result of these operations PERONNE was shortly afterwards occupied by the 143rd Bde & the Division holds the line of the SOMME CANAL to S of PERONNE.	
ACHILLE VALLEY			The Battalion remained in present area & [illegible] Coys 7th Worcs on right & 4th Glos on left pushed thro' to [illegible] Outpost Line to cover Division at front with Patrols to push forward [illegible] back to ACHILLE VALLEY.	HYC
	19-20		Bn employed on [illegible] & road making	HYC
FLAUCOURT & HERBECOURT	21		Bn [illegible] HQ [illegible] neighbourhood of the Bde HQ [illegible] FLAUCOURT. 'A' [illegible] FLAUCOURT	HYC
	22		[illegible] HERBECOURT [illegible] Nord	
			Working parties continued on road making & bridging in newly acquired area around PERONNE.	
PERONNE	27	8 pm	Bn moved to [illegible] billets in RUE MOLLERUE PERONNE.	HYC
	28		Working parties [illegible] on road repairs	HYC
HAMEL	29	10 am	Bn moved to HAMEL (62c NE [illegible] K13c) billeted in houses [illegible] by refugees, billets very dirty.	HYC
	30		Coys employed on cleaning houses & cellars to provide further accommodation.	HYC
VILLERS FAUCON	31	7.30 pm	A Coy moved to VILLERS-FAUCON to be attached to 2nd [illegible] who had attacked STE EMILIE at 4 pm	HYC
		10.30 pm	Bn less A Coy moved to LONGAVESNES where they halted until 8.30 pm they then proceeded out to take over	
		8.30	the outpost line from the 2nd [illegible] in front of VILLERS-FAUCON along the line of the railway K5c to E29b then in front of STE EMILIE. Bn on left 7th Worcs. Bn on right 2/4 Lincs 59th Div	HYC

H Y Clarke Major Comdg 1/8 Worc Regt

A5834 Wt. W4973/M687 750,000 8/16 D. D. & L. Ltd. Forms/C.2118/13.

Afghanistan
War Diary
No. 120 to No. 136 from 16.11.79 to 30.11.79
(Vol XXIV)

Army Form C. 2118.

WAR DIARY
or
INTELLIGENCE SUMMARY
(Erase heading not required.)

1/8th Bn The Worcestershire Regt

Instructions regarding War Diaries and Intelligence Summaries are contained in F.S. Regs., Part II. and the Staff Manual respectively. Title pages will be prepared in manuscript.

Place	Date 1917	Hour	Summary of Events and Information	Remarks and references to Appendices
VILLERS FAUCON	April 1		2nd anniversary of landing in FRANCE. Battalion had rum & bigus [biscuits] issued forward. Patrolled the MAY COPSE – RONSSOY WOOD. B Coy on right beyond TEMPLEUX WOOD. B Coy	WD
	2	11th 6.30am	A platoon of B Coy went as a strong fighting patrol toward LEMPIRE; a Platoon of C Coy advanced at the same time and forward to RONSSOY to find if villages were strongly held. The enemy found to hold RONSSOY in force. B Coy ?, C Coy ?	WD
		10am	Casualties A few C, D, nil B	
	3	4.15 PM	Rea [Relieved] by 1/4 Ox & Bucks LI. Bn returned to billets at TINCOURT area in 1.30am. Bn moved to	WD WD
TINCOURT	4		Coy at about midday it was intimated to the CO that the Bn would attack the KOWO + Quarry in F29 Cd [L3 ark] and the Spur in F29 Cd and L9a NE of TEMPLEUX-LE-GUERARD. Definite orders were not received to write this attack until 11 PM. In the opinion the CO and Company Commanders reconnoitred the ground and preliminary	WD
	5		orders issued. Bn attacked H30 and C.A 15 b d. The 1/5 Bn attacked SONAEY at 4.45 AM & Coy of the 1/8 Bn were sent to protect the flank at 6.55 am at what time the enemy opened a heavy rifle and MG fire from his top line trenches. Coy under RUEORY and LANY to climb a long steep slope. Reached top of the hill just back the enemy were found to hold ABEL RUEORY and a certain extent LANY. Captain Bate and 150 and odd rank in to [sic] Runry Suffered heavy casualties...	WD

Army Form C. 2118.

Instructions regarding War Diaries and Intelligence Summaries are contained in F. S. Regs., Part II. and the Staff Manual respectively. Title pages will be prepared in manuscript.

WAR DIARY
or
INTELLIGENCE SUMMARY.

(Erase heading not required.) 1/8th Bn The Worcestershire Regt

Place	Date	Hour	Summary of Events and Information	Remarks and references to Appendices
	April 1917		The enemy left 9 dead and 1 wounded and 2 unwounded prisoners. They also suffered other casualties during the fight for the minnie which it is not necessary to mention here. Bn HQ & the 2 companies were relieved and the work of consolidation began. Our casualties: officers (1 Lt important) + 11 OR killed, 37 OR wounded and 1 officer + 47 Rwndg. Bn was relieved at 3 pm by 59th Bde in Coan Gully. Arrangements were made for Commander in Chief and for C in C and Lt Col O Reserve to know experience of VLG, 40C Oct and 13¼ General.	mm
Tincourt	6		Sun & Monday. On 8th a Military Funeral service was held and the men before burial in the mil. Cemetery in attendance. Capt & Lt Majors, Capt Thomson, Lieut Ratcliffe & 2/Lt Luke, 2/Lt Reynolds.	mm
Villers Faucon	7		Orders received from Brigade this day to proceed with attack on Villers Faucon. Bn men coming for instruction many approaches from Tincourt, Hervilly Ronsoy to Tincourt & Roisel are L & O. Staff VILLERS FAUCON 2 markings of an approach & ... also there Lt then its	mm
		2 PM		mm
		5.30 PM	Bn Cyclists report 8.30 P.M.	mm

Army Form C. 2118.

WAR DIARY
or
INTELLIGENCE SUMMARY.
(Erase heading not required.)

1/8th Bn The Worcestershire Reg

Place	Date 1917 April	Hour	Summary of Events and Information	Remarks and references to Appendices
VILLERS FAUCON	8		Working Parties. Coy Hd Qrs and Coys in VILLERS FAUCON — ROISEL and VILLERS FAUCON — LONGAVESNES roads. Working Party 200 O.R. for Tunnelling officer at VILLERS FAUCON.	Im
"	9		Working Party — 100 from A+D. Much as day before B.O. arrived back from leave.	Im
"			2/Lt Lee now attd 4th Glosc' Lts. Outpost line from ROISEL — BOULOGNE to HARGICOURT. C+D from line. A+B support. ROISEL WOOD in reserve.	
			H.Q. at TEMPLEUX WOOD	
TEMPLEUX WOOD	10		Patrols out & Situation of ground in vicinity of outpost line.	Im
"	11		Coys H.Q. & 2 Coys (B Coy) pushed forward to take X roads at F 20 b 05. 2 other Coys (the 5th lines) also pushed forward on our right to take the LAGER FARM. Both coys lost their way and emerged so far southward that the lines beyond our front and support lines. Our objective was gained (our casuals 1 officer 4 OR) The matter of 2nd line Coy could not be ascertained but it is certain they lost a good number. Lt Jones lost hardly and failed to take their objective. With the result that our right flank at X roads was left very much in air. We returned by Ad. Wares. Relief completed 12 P.M.	Im

11.

Army Form C. 2118.

WAR DIARY
or
INTELLIGENCE SUMMARY
(Erase heading not required.)

1/8 Bn The Worcestershire Regt

Place	Date 1917	Hour	Summary of Events and Information	Remarks and references to Appendices
VILLERS FAUCON	April 12		Bn moved into cellars etc at VILLERS FAUCON. Bn split in Cleary and resting at 10.30 PM received orders to be ready to move at 10 minutes notice after 4 am, to support 4th Wores in attack. Men kept in full boots on.	mn
	13		4th did not required. 4th Wores having attained objective. Working party moved under R.E. at dump 4/5 VILLERS FAUCON. Bm inspected by 1/4 Royal Berks and march back to TINCOURT. Bm orders chiefly of regress instead by CO. Bm arrived in billets in 6.30 PM	mn
TINCOURT	14	6.30am	Working party of 2 Centuries under RE at TINCOURT. Bn b at TINCOURT detailed to be duty morning	mn
	15		Working party of 1 century under RE at TINCOURT. Battn for manoeuvre of Bn	mn
Camp near ROISEL	16		Left TINCOURT for camp in sunken cutting near ROISEL K11. Here the Bn were in Divisional Reserve and was warned to be in readiness to support 145 Bde to their attack	mn
	17	4am	At 4 AM Bn were ordered to 'stand to' - working parties were carried on. Bn stood to the whole day.	mn
	18		A & B Coys lessons musketry parades. C & D Coys Res Gas lectures to officers and gas N.C.Os by Divisional Gas officer Capt Trapnell	mn

Army Form C. 2118.

WAR DIARY
or
INTELLIGENCE SUMMARY. 1/8th Bn. The Worcestershire Reg t

(Erase heading not required.)

Instructions regarding War Diaries and Intelligence Summaries are contained in F. S. Regs., Part II. and the Staff Manual respectively. Title pages will be prepared in manuscript.

Place	Date	Hour	Summary of Events and Information	Remarks and references to Appendices
Ravine near Monchy	April 1917 19		Intelligence Officer and O.C. companies went forward to reconnoitre forward area (F11 & 18, 23 & 24) in front of GILLEMONT FARM. The O.C.s and Coy's who were leading them were to take GILLEMONT FARM and be relieved by us the same night. Their attack however failed. We relieved them in their original line.	
Cutting East from X roads Fins to Fins	20	4.30 AM	Battalion in G + 30 AM. A regiment "B" Left, "C" Support. It was intended by the C.O. that the Bn. would be ready to attack on GILLEMONT FARM should there be much resistance. If the Coy. were down and a form for Bn. HQ was sited in trench (the Sunken Road at F22)	
Camp East Fins			Bn. relieved by 48th West. Relay complete about 9.30 PM. Bn. marched back to Camp 2 companies at HQ at E29 & A C + D companies at F25a.	
	22		Church Parade. The day mainly used for cleaning up etc. O.C.'s B. Co. & A.D.C.'s had been given an order to practice forward Coys in night attack and captured GILLEMONT FARM E saps m A 3 Coy between and open work found in A1dd (Blue print 64C HE 16.2.4 NU) Permanent guides taken round area	

Army Form C. 2118.

WAR DIARY
or
INTELLIGENCE SUMMARY.
(Erase heading not required.) 1/8th Bn The Worcestershire Regt

Instructions regarding War Diaries and Intelligence Summaries are contained in F. S. Regs., Part II. and the Staff Manual respectively. Title pages will be prepared in manuscript.

Place	Date	Hour	Summary of Events and Information	Remarks and references to Appendices
	1917 April 22	11.30 AM	Preparations commenced. Final operation orders were completed at about 12.30 A.M. Outline of operations were as follows:- B Coy 140 to form at A19d.12 on road NE of GILLEMONT FARM & road at A13b36 inclusive. D Coy with two platoons of A – Road at A13b36 inclusive to A19d to form two centre cross tracks in F24d. A Coy in support of B Coy on ground in A19d. B Coy was in support scanning sunken road and front line between road and A coy. B moved off at 11.45 – B Coy got astray onto the line, it attacking in fairs hardly waiting in the Garrison F27 Coy returns from Ration.	1pm
	24	1.15 AM	at 1 AM A Coy started full of finesse when informed by C10 and continuing marched there known and deployed into two attacking formations under heavier and artillery fire.	
		3.45 AM	at 3.15 AM the attack commenced 10 mins after when in answer to signal lights the enemy artillery started. In addition to rifle and MG fire, from the front at our front were covered in and less by Capt Prosser they charged the two company front the infantry who suffered heavy	1pm

Army Form C. 2118.

14

WAR DIARY
or
~~INTELLIGENCE SUMMARY.~~
(Erase heading not required.) 1/8th Bn The Worcestershire Regt

Place	Date	Hour	Summary of Events and Information	Remarks and references to Appendices
	1917 April/24 cont		casualties as they ran back. German officer was found wounded and dressed by one stretcher bearer. 1 M.G. captured and stronger reinft. parties consolidation began at once. The tractors on the right attempting the capture A19a were held up. Men again attempting in vain to meet remnants of Tanks were withdrawn to organise line. C+D above on left failed to take their objective with the result that C+D were exposed on both flanks. for several hrs the Pl 6th D led by 2/Lt Pittard + Capt Plowdowe, and a remnant of the 144 Bde M.G. Company continued to do excellent work against the enemy in their two tanks but the left attack against the knoll having failed the ground gained was untenable. The enemy prevented this. with Infantry + combined attack. This combined attack was driven off with M.G, L.G fire. At 4.57 AM the enemy put in another counter attack was launched a new Infantry army and although unable to keep the enemy at bay our own wriggly to retire about 9 o'clock. Position was forced to retire about 9 o'clock.	WW
		4 AM	Our casualties were killed - Capt Tommy, Capt Plowdowe, Lieut Sweeley, Lieut Dimbleton, wounded - Lewis Pittard, Bomford + Saton. Injured + Missing Lieut Potter. Missing believed killed or Prisoners O.R. killed 15, missing 65, wounds 1, wounded 64. wounded at duty 1.	WW

A 534 Wt W4973/M637 730000 8/16 D.D & L Ltd. forms/C.2118/13.

Army Form C. 2118.

WAR DIARY
or
INTELLIGENCE SUMMARY. 1/8th Bn. The Worcestershire Regt.

(Erase heading not required.)

Instructions regarding War Diaries and Intelligence Summaries are contained in F. S. Regs., Part II. and the Staff Manual respectively. Title pages will be prepared in manuscript.

Place	Date 1917	Hour	Summary of Events and Information	Remarks and references to Appendices
	April 24 cont		Missing 63 Bn. relieved by 1/4th Worc. and Royal Berks - C/HQ 15 camp in F25 c, A+B Coys holding sunken road TOINE WOOD and strong points on Brown line. HQ at old Bn. HQ in F27.	Wh
	April 25		Bn. relieved by Ox & Bucks and moved to HAMEL. Relief complete about 8.30 PM	Wh
HAMEL	26		A+B baths at TINCOURT. Day spent in resting, relieving. C.O. inspected new draft of 35.	Wh
	27		C, D + HQ details baths at TINCOURT. Been working parties in woods at MARQUAIX. Company parade for close order drill & rifle inspection.	Wh
K 5 central	28		Coy working party in woods at MARQUAIX. Companies continue training. Bn. relieved by 1st Worc. Relief complete 4.30 P.M. before leaving. Tummy & Plantiere. Lt Lentzbuck, Lt. Morton, Pte Ropley, Hughes, interred at L.1.d.99. A service was conducted by Rev. J.B. Ford C.F. and attended by C.O. and all available officers.	Wh
Outpost line from A17d to A29c	29		Weather delightful. Church parade at 10.30 A.M. attended by General Farebrace GOC 48 Division. Bn. relieve 1/4 Ox & Bucks - taking over the outpost line from A17d to A29c. Relief complete about 11.30 P.M. C at GILLEMONT FARM, B Support in QUEBECHETTES WOOD + F17d. B centre - F23c + F23b d. A right F29c b.	Wh
	30		Very quiet except for aeroplane activity. Weather very fine.	Wh

Nolan Lt. Col.
Comdg. 1/8 Bn. The Worc. Regt.

Copy/extracts

War Diary
of
The Worcestershire Regt.

1st May to 31st May 1911

(Vol. XXVI)

Army Form C. 2118.

WAR DIARY
or
INTELLIGENCE SUMMARY.
(Erase heading not required.)

1/8th Bn. The Worcestershire Regt.

Instructions regarding War Diaries and Intelligence Summaries are contained in F. S. Regs., Part II. and the Staff Manual respectively. Title pages will be prepared in manuscript.

Place	Date 1917	Hour	Summary of Events and Information	Remarks and references to Appendices
Map FRANCE 62a sheet Outpost line A7d to A27c.	May 1		Fine weather continued. Bn. relieved by 1/5 Lanc. Fusiliers of 42nd Division. Relief complete 11.30 P.M. Bn. marches back to camp at K5 central.	Map FRANCE 62a 1/40000.
			A few men detailed in CLEMONT FARM. (J.PBATE)	Mr
Isolated	2		Day spent in cleaning and resting. Capts Pate & Pawsey granted leave to M.C. Sergt Edwards & Cpl Eastburn awarded D.C.M.	Mr
BUIRE	3	8 A.M.	Bn. marches to camp at BUIRE arrived there 10.15 A.M. Cars being again from FLIXECOURT.	Mr
	4		Training. Ceremonial Parade and presentation of D.C.M. to Sgt Edwards & Cpl Eastburn. C.O. read out on parade the letter upon which they were granted and also the letter upon which the bars to the M.C. were granted to Capts Pate & Pawsey.	Mr
	5		Rainy school started. Major Scott Q.M. goes on leave.	Mr
	6		Training continued. Combined Church Parade with 6th Gloucesters. attended by Brigadier Genl. Reading, shortly for officers.	Mr
	7		O.C. returns from leave. A+B working parties. Baths at TINCOURT	Mr

Army Form C. 2118.

WAR DIARY
or
INTELLIGENCE SUMMARY.

(Erase heading not required.)

1/8th Bn. The Worcestershire Regt.

Instructions regarding War Diaries and Intelligence Summaries are contained in F.S. Regs., Part II. and the Staff Manual respectively. Title pages will be prepared in manuscript.

Place	Date 1917	Hour	Summary of Events and Information	Remarks and references to Appendices
BUIRE 62c J27.	May 7		C.O. & 2nd in Command go for Staff ride with G.O.C. Duvoir. Training of NCOs in the evening.	MAP FRANCE 62c 1/40000
"	8		Change of weather - strong wind, rain. Kit inspection in morning. Training in afternoon.	"
"	9		The Bn. was set a Tactical Exercise by Brigade. The idea was that Division was under orders to take the high ground opposite TINCOURT in J16 & J22 b & d. The Bn. had for its front objective the high ground reported to be in J21. The C.O. and officers examined reconnoitred the ground and discussed mode of dealing with the situation.	
"	10	9am	Bn. exercised the Tactical Exercise. The Brigadier was in attendance & men were tested as enemy. Two companies in fire-line - each company in two waves, two platoons in each wave. Training continued in the afternoon.	"
"	11		A, B & C working parties under R.E. D Coy & Specialists continue training. Got no information there. Bn. is likely to move following morning so training to discontinue & men are warned to keep in camp in case of Bele [Bells?]	"
"	12	4pm	Bn. goes Red - Bivouac hand to attendance. Bn. marched to PERONE where it was billeted for the night.	"

WAR DIARY
or
INTELLIGENCE SUMMARY
1/8th Bn. The Worcestershire Regt.

(Erase heading not required.)

Army Form C. 2118.

Place	Date 1917	Hour	Summary of Events and Information	Remarks and references to Appendices
COMBLES Map FRANCE 57c 1/40000	May 13	4.45 AM	144 Bde headed by 1/8th Bn Worc Regt marched to COMBLES and	Map FRANCE 57c 1/40000
		9. AM.	Bde arrived at COMBLES and to entertained by Lt. General Pulteney Commanding III Corps. He also presented ribbons to the men to whom they had been awarded.	
LE TRANSLOY VILLERS-au-FLOS N30 c/7	14	3.50 AM	Under very bad conditions of road marched Bn. start to VILLERS-au-FLOS via LE TRANSLOY. At VILLERS Bn. had breakfast & dinner. Packs were dumped and the Bn. commenced	
		2.30 PM	march to VELU at 2.30 P.M. Here the Bn. relieved the 6th Yorkshire Regt in Bivouacs round, which was A & B Coys. shot L & E Coys a Coys. dug outs at J36 a 58, Q8 c 8, J27 b 84. Bn. H.Q. J9 a 97. The whole march from PERONNE & VELU in the W of the march from PERONNE & VELU was very trying for the men they however stood it very well, only one fell out + this man [in] the hands of the doctor before we started	
VELU J31 d0	15		Day spent in cleaning mate.	
	16		Improvement of Camp, training of Lewis Gunners and Reserve Signallers. 6 O.T.2nd in Command most night support Bn. Raining very heavily.	

19

Army Form C. 2118.

WAR DIARY
or
INTELLIGENCE SUMMARY
1/8th Bn. The Worcestershire Regt.
(Erase heading not required.)

Place	Date 1917	Hour	Summary of Events and Information	Remarks and references to Appendices
VELU Map 57c FRANCE 1/31	May 17		Physical Training. Coys. train for an hour. Training of Lewis Gunners & Reserve Sigs. Improvement of Lewis Gun trenches during night. Working party of 200 men for night work under R.E. digging trenches during afternoon (8.30 P.M. till Dawn).	Map - FRANCE 57c 1/40000 mu
Do	18		Working party for night work as yesterday.	mu
Do	19		Physical training. German aeroplane shot down by Corpl. Lisbourne and then seen in Hamincourt Wood. The aeroplane fell down in the 20th Divisional Area. The observer was killed with pilot wounded. The G.O.C. Division sent a telegram of congratulation and ordered the hole other orth unit wounded men 'have a drink'. The men who had not received their turkish out the hand of Lunar Jamboree which refused to attend a Church Parade held at FREMICOURT (1.25) Company officers. L.9. T Sigs off went forward to get particulars of the Lilac Line.	mu mu mu mu
Do	20			
LOUVERVAL OUTPOST LINE D.29.c & D.29.d	21		Bn leaves VELU 8.30 P.M. for outpost line moving from N.22 & N. to D.29.c. The whole day at VELU was marked by heavy shelling of VELU WOOD and the results there another	mu

WAR DIARY or INTELLIGENCE SUMMARY

1/8th Bn. The Worcestershire Regt.

Army Form C. 2118.

Place	Date 1917	Hour	Summary of Events and Information	Remarks and references to Appendices
LOUVERVAL OUTPOST LINE Boursies Dozed & Vaux 57c	May 22.		route of departure fixed to be selected. Relief complete about 1 A.M. trenches turned out very wet. Rain poured down throughout the night. Disposition A Coy Right front, C Centre, D Left front, B in support. The front line was made up of detached trenches. The companies in front had 3 platoons in front line and 1 platoon in support and Coy H.Q., 3 Pltns in front. Each company had 3 L.G's in front line. Casualty 1 – slight wound in head from A.A. gun. Bn on left 1/4th Hldrs Home Regt; 1 Bn. on right 1/4th Bn. Oxf. & Bucks L.I.	War Map FRANCE 57c
	23		2 Lewis Guns & 2 Grenadiers L.G. units of the enemy night attack to reduce pressure were discussed & arranged – the companies being so thinly manned. It was finally decided to hold the front line with 2 companies and 2 Coys in reserve. Strong patrols were sent out which orders to offer if necessary no signs yet seen however.	more

Army Form C. 2118.

WAR DIARY
or
INTELLIGENCE SUMMARY.
1/8th Bn. The Worcestershire Regt

(Erase heading not required.)

Instructions regarding War Diaries and Intelligence Summaries are contained in F. S. Regs., Part II. and the Staff Manual respectively. Title pages will be prepared in manuscript.

Place	Date	Hour	Summary of Events and Information	Remarks and references to Appendices
OUTPOST LINE	May 1917 24		Day very fine – aeroplanes very active. New dispositions were carried out – D & A in front line and C & B in reserve. A night front; D left front; Lieut H.S. BENJAMIN rejoined Battalion right support; B left support from England. Two patrols went out again but found nothing.	Map FRANCE 57c
Doret to Dase	25.		Generally quiet weather fine. B relieves D in front line.	
	26.		Very quiet – weather fine. Casualty 1 wounded. Four reconnoitring patrols in charge of N.C.Os. Nothing was seen of the enemy.	
	27.		Capt. J.P. Bate returned from leave. (a months absence) 6 coy relieves A in front line. 5 officer patrols again went out but nothing was seen of patrols or enemy.	
	28.		A strong officers patrol was sent out from right company to take trench in D 2.w.c. The patrol consisted of 2 platoons which two flank guards of 1 section each. The trench was found unoccupied Patrol returned 2.15 A.M. Bn relieved by 1/7 Royal Warwicks. Relief complete about 1:30 A.M. Bn marched back to VÉLU.	
VÉLU	29.		Day spent in cleaning trench. 2Lt J.H. CLARK from Reserve Bn. reported for duty.	soon
	30		Bn had the South of VÉLU & clean was nothing.	
	31			

J. A. Lee V.A.M.
commanding 1/8 = the Worc. Regt.

Confidential

Vol 27

War Diary of Worcestershire Regt (T.F.)

for June 30th June 1914

(Vol. XXVII)

Army Form C. 2118.

WAR DIARY
or
INTELLIGENCE SUMMARY 1/8th Bn. The Worcestershire Regt.
(Erase heading not required.)

Instructions regarding War Diaries and Intelligence Summaries are contained in F.S. Regs., Part II. and the Staff Manual respectively. Title pages will be prepared in manuscript.

Place	Date	Hour	Summary of Events and Information	Remarks and references to Appendices
VELU J.31	JUNE 1		144th INF. BDE in Divisional Reserve. The Battalion encamped in VELU WOOD, and carried on training in accordance with programme. Engaged in training. Musketry, Bayonet Fighting and Company Fighting in general were practised.	MAP REFERENCE 57c J.31 1/10,000 57c J.16 1/40,000
	2		Lt Col H. CARR D.S.O. was appointed to command and the 144 Inf. Bde in temporary absence of Brig Gen H. R. DONE D.S.O. – Major H. T. CLARKE assumed command of the Battalion. Divine Service parade in VELU CHATEAU GROUNDS.	57c J.16
	3	10 A.M.	Working parties were found. Bio-Strong, from an BEAUMETZ-MORCHIES LINE, returning at 4-30 A.M.	57c J.16
		9.30 P.M. 11.45 P.M.	A gas attack was carried out at STRONG Boy. Bombs being exploded and ... attempt in enemy's lines. It was put attended to be a false one. It is believed the Bon signals ... the enemy sending up Golden Rain rockets prior to our gas. Officer noticed ... B coy was inspected by G.O.C. training continued. A.B.C. Coys were inspected G.O.C. in the afternoon. In the ... battalion tended & presentation of medals awarded to officers the attack of GUILLEMONT FARM on 8-1-17.	57c J.16
	4 5	3 P.M.		57c J.16
	6	9.30 A.M.	2/Lt G.M. JONES received the Military Cross at a parade HQ 144TH INF.BDE WOODWARD TO BIENVILLERS CROIX DE GUERRE. Battalion again returned to "B" Reconnaissance RLt. R.F. Post Price, 2nd Lt R. Barlett of Left Brigade. – Rest of days was spent in making 2/Lts G.H.E. Hosp. 42 came in to ... field that title, Returns & ... were ... and heavy... ... D Coy left Reserve... "A" Coy left in Country Right Reserve. 1/4 Bn. Stevedore. 2/L on our Right 35 1/6 B. Stevedore RGT. Another Bn. HQ LOUVERVAL J.10-5.85-40 on our left.	57c J.16

WAR DIARY
or
INTELLIGENCE SUMMARY.

(Erase heading not required.)

1/8th Bn. The Worcestershire Regt.

Army Form C. 2118.

Instructions regarding War Diaries and Intelligence Summaries are contained in F. S. Regs., Part II. and the Staff Manual respectively. Title pages will be prepared in manuscript.

Place	Date	Hour	Summary of Events and Information	Remarks and references to Appendices
	7		Two small patrols went out. One was ordered to reconnoitre LOUVERVAL-PETIT between 350 c.c.d H30 on SUNKEN ROAD in J.14.a and LOUVERVAL. C.S.M. HEYDON	3176
	8		was killed in SUNKEN ROAD J14.a.6.7 outskirts of J.14.a.9.9 & the Rev FRITH from 1st St. He was carried down during night to aid station. Some men wounded — patrols went out	3176
	9		Enemy shelled pattering front line during day. D.14.37, D.28.6.20, J.14.6.55. Posn lie Day nil. Two strong patrols went out during night to reconnoitre Normay and and enemy trenches in Right coy. D30.6.19, D23.b.9. Posn lie D.23.b.40 to D.23.b.11. Left coy.	3176
	10		Suffn lines and LOUVERVAL at estimated D22.d, D23.a. Two patrols sent out before daybreak. Enemy posted following areas D.22.b, D.22.c.7.5 a patrol returned report C.14.51.	3176
	11		Enemy shelled D23.b, J.14.a, J.10a, D23b at night during day C27.50.45	3176
	12		fell on CATEBRAI ROAD J.14.d — catapult shown gully fors grenades at junction of gullies at D30.b.03. Twelve dead Germans who fired 8" mortar J.14.5.E. D30.c.07. Enemy night barrel mortar fish patrol returned 250 am.	3176
	13		Enemy cut fifty leads in. GRANATENWERFER was fired at half L.B.2 (unreadable) at D30.d.69. 2 Lieut BAMFORD and 4 others patrolled down gully between crater at D30.b.66. heavy mg fire along Hostile D-25. D24.d.21. gathering no casualties.	3176
	14		Out posts were known D-5.a mortars fire Bay at shelter for C coy to be handed over to 1/7 Right Mow S.K.L. Pt. n. Resist.	3176

[A7092] Wt. W18599/M 1293 75,000 4/17. D. D. & L., Ltd. Forms/C.2118/14.

WAR DIARY
or
INTELLIGENCE SUMMARY.   1/8th Bn. The Worcestershire Regt.

(Erase heading not required.)

Army Form C. 2118.

Place	Date	Hour	Summary of Events and Information	Remarks and references to Appendices
LOUVERAL	14		A trench 20×6×4 was dug at D29 c.4.2, one 50×2×4 at D28 d.8.4, one 40× feng at D29 central and another D29 c.12	MAP FRANCE 57C 1:40,000 WY6
VELU	15		Relief complete at 2 AM. Return to camp in VELU WOOD effective. Bath at VELU and change of underclothing. MILITARY CROSS awarded to CAPT W.F. LOTTON (144 I.F. Bde. Staff Captain) and 2.LT. S.H. WIKES. Intain economy etc.	WY6
	16			WY6
	17	7 a.m.	C.O. with Company officers reconn'd 7 to reflect gun in attack P.FESTRY scheme, also assault course (Bayonet fighting) and bombing ground.	WY6
	18	11.30 AM	2 Lt. that parade. 2 Lt. QUINLAN and 1fto reinforcement, inspected by Bty. Commanding Officer. Training was continued to be carried out between 6 AM & 10 a.m. and 6 P.M. & 8 P.M. on account of the heat.	WY6
	19		2nd Lt. M. H. A. CARR D.S.O. relinquished command of B.Sig.S. and assumed command 57 Battalion.	WY6
	20		A tactical scheme was carried out by B Battalion. Brig Gen. HEADLAM D.S.O. Brig. Comdt. He had an Option of the exercises in being later carried out by forces attached (not less than 5).	WY6
	21		Training continued according to programme.	WY6
	22	9.30 P.M.	Battalion relieved 1/7 & 3 Rgt. to main S.S. Regt Lift line as before. Relief VELU 12.30 AM (23). MAJOR CLARKE assumed command 23rd. 8/63.	WY6
	23		Relief complete 12.30 AM (23).	WY6
	24		Situation very quiet, most take clean patrols during a tour of front came signs of activity.	WY6

WAR DIARY
or
INTELLIGENCE SUMMARY.
(Erase heading not required.)

Army Form C. 2118.

1/8th Bn. The Worcestershire Regt

Instructions regarding War Diaries and Intelligence Summaries are contained in F. S. Regs., Part II. and the Staff Manual respectively. Title pages will be prepared in manuscript.

Place	Date	Hour	Summary of Events and Information	Remarks and references to Appendices
LOUVERVAL	24		Section of sentries relieved the R.E. material & the strength up to Centipede not taken instead of carrying them down. Should have occupied it.	MAP Reference 57c N.W. 1:40,000 J.H.Y.C.
	25		A patrol of 3 men and 2/Lt Barford & 2/Lt Clark went out by Gully to wire at D20 b08. Met by enemy patrol - advanced to about 30 yds - fired at with rifle, Lewis guns at with grenades. Hit was taken by 2/Lt no casualties on the way in & Capt Raynes on attempt to advance.	J.H.Y.C.
	26		2/Lt Baker & Ptes of guard patrolling C. trench. Later 5/4 Gloucestershire Regt to whom we handed over trench reported that patrol retired in confusion was fired at by patrol & few where mentioned.	J.H.Y.C.
			Reported by 5/4 Glos on main a patrol of 5 Germans went out from D29 c13 bombed our trench & 50 m.g. bullets. Rifle reported enemy lost dead German bodies to identification.	J.H.Y.C.
	27		Intro - Coy by Coy relief for D Coy (LEFT) was relieved by B Coy LEFT Reserves, Pitoing them into A Coy (Right) relieved by C Coy Right Reserves, and nice cross. During relief the M.O. Capt MARTIN D.S.O. was killed by shell which fell on a cellar.	J.H.Y.C.
	28		LOUVERVAL shelled at 7.30 150 HV shells falling in and around it from left to right. from Cafe chen b.6.Se. (2)	J.H.Y.C.
	29		Suft trench at D29 c28 and D28 b41 shelled with action at 10.42	J.H.Y.C.
	30		Night 29/30 bombards Verlet Catelet b.6.Se.	J.H.Y.C.

J.H. Colcombe
Commanding 1/8th Bn. Worcestershire Regt.

Confidential

War Diary
of
Headquarters Boyce (TF)

From 1st July to 31st July 1944

(Vol. XXVIII)

Army Form C. 2118.
26.

Instructions regarding War Diaries and Intelligence
Summaries are contained in F. S. Regs., Part II.
and the Staff Manual respectively. Title pages
will be prepared in manuscript.

WAR DIARY
or
INTELLIGENCE SUMMARY.
(Erase heading not required.)

1/8th Bn. The Worcestershire Regt.

Place	Date 1917	Hour	Summary of Events and Information	Remarks and references to Appendices
LOUVERVAL	July 1	9.10pm	Officers of 8th E. Yorks came up to reconnoitre trenches	mu
	2		Unusual aerial activity on part of enemy	mu
LOUVERVAL FREMICOURT ACHIET-LE-PETIT	3		Bn relieved in trenches by 8th E. Yorks, Relief complete. Bn marched to FREMICOURT Bn marched to ACHIET-LE-PETIT starting at 2.0m. The battn. entraining and alont 60 men fell out	mu
ACHIET LE PETIT MONCHY	4	6.30am	Bn arrived at ACHIET-LE-PETIT Bn moved to MONCHY	mu
MONCHY	5	8 am	Provisional tactical scheme for Bn Staff	mu
		7.30pm	MONCHY being out of Bn area, Bn was moved to ADINFER	
ADINFER	6	9 am	ADINFER condemned by M.O. held mistaken steps to return to MONCHY	mu
MONCHY		8.30am	Bn moved to MONCHY	mu
MONCHY	7		Provisional scheme carried out by 144 Inf. Bde.	mu
	8		Holiday — very wet	mu
	9		Training of companies and specialists	mu

Army Form C. 2118.
27

WAR DIARY
or
INTELLIGENCE SUMMARY.
(Erase heading not required.)

1/8th Bn. The Worcestershire Regt.

Instructions regarding War Diaries and Intelligence Summaries are contained in F.S. Regs., Part II. and the Staff Manual respectively. Title pages will be prepared in manuscript.

Place	Date 1917 July	Hour	Summary of Events and Information	Remarks and references to Appendices
MONCHY	10		Training continued. 2/Lt H.C. BROWN joined Bn. for duty, and appointed Intelligence Officer	mm
"	11		Training continued. Draft of 145 O.R. received — men chiefly from 7th Norfolk Rgt., of good physique and well trained in musketry etc.; but soft for marching	mm
"	12		Training continued. Reinoculation of Bn. commenced	mm
"	13		Training continued. Reinoculation completed	mm
"	14		Training continued. A, B, & 2/Lts of C Coy held friendly Match	mm
"	15		Letter by Capt J.P. BATE on the command of a Battalion of BLAIREVILLE Battalion Horse Show. at BLAIREVILLE. Following chargers:— Firsts for best pair of light Draught in lines, Best Pair of light Draught in harness (within 1 light Draught) Best Pair of heavy hunters (within 1 light Draught) Best Pair of Pack Animals in harness (within 1 Pack Animal in harness). Seconds for pair of mules, hunter, pair of Pack Animals in harness; Thirds for pair of heavy Draught & hunter. Officers charger also got a 3rd for N.C.O.'s horse. Draft of 58 O.R. arrived, partly trained	mm
	16		144 of above took part in Bde Scheme attacking DOUCHY eN AYETTE.	mm

Army Form C. 2118.

28

WAR DIARY
or
INTELLIGENCE SUMMARY.
(Erase heading not required.)

1/8th Bn. The Worcestershire Regt.

Instructions regarding War Diaries and Intelligence Summaries are contained in F. S. Regs., Part II. and the Staff Manual respectively. Title pages will be prepared in manuscript.

Place	Date 1917 July	Hour	Summary of Events and Information	Remarks and references to Appendices
MONCHY	14		Training continued by Companies and Specialists	hm
"	18		Battalion Scheme	hm
"	19		2 Pltns of C Coy & D Coy - field firing. Training continued	hm
"	20		No late news and advance orders for battalion on 22nd received	hm
"	21		Training continued	hm
"	22	1.30PM	Bn moved via BIENVILLERS - PONNIER - HUMBERCAMPS to SAULTY - LARBRET Station and there entrained. State 24 officers 264 OR 65 animals 23 vehicles 9 bicycles	hm
"		9.0PM	Train started	hm
POPERINGHE	23	5.10AM	Bn detrained at HOPOUTRE and marched 2 miles to billets in the vicinity of the Square, POPERINGHE	hm
"	24		Training continued by Conferences and Specialists	hm
"	25		Training continued. Model of forward area visited	hm
"	26		Training continued	hm
"	27		Training continued. Rev. J.G. BYRNE C.F. arrived to take the place of Rev. J.B. FRITH proceeding to 14 P.B.D. CALAIS for duty.	hm
"	28		Training continued. Lt R.W. STEVESON and 5 OR formed the latter officer posted K.A.C.S.	hm

Army Form C. 2118.

WAR DIARY
or
INTELLIGENCE SUMMARY.

(Erase heading not required.) 1/8th Bn. The Worcestershire Regt.

Instructions regarding War Diaries and Intelligence Summaries are contained in F. S. Regs., Part II. and the Staff Manual respectively. Title pages will be prepared in manuscript.

Place	Date 1917	Hour	Summary of Events and Information	Remarks and references to Appendices
POPERINGHE	29 July	4 AM	C.O. Coy Comdrs & bn Staff reconoitre ground east of CANAL (Map Belgium 28)	
	30		Training continued	
	31	8·10 AM	Bn. moved forward to Camp. C. at A 29 c.11. ~ Transport moves in the afternoon to field adjoining	
			Medical details on Corp/11 Front	Medium full Annex 18 the war Diary

Confidential

War Diary
of
Wat Pat Wawanesa Ry

From 1/7/44 to 31/8/44

(Vol XXIX)

Army Form C. 2118.

WAR DIARY
or
INTELLIGENCE SUMMARY.

(Erase heading not required.)

1/8th Bn. The Worcestershire Regt.

Instructions regarding War Diaries and Intelligence Summaries are contained in F. S. Regs., Part II. and the Staff Manual respectively. Title pages will be prepared in manuscript.

Place	Date	Hour	Summary of Events and Information	Remarks and references to Appendices
BRAKE CAMP	13		Coy. training. Cpt. killed during night, an Officer & ninety wounded.	J/P43
	14		Reflation. Strow economy section opening of section [?] and Coy Training	J/P43
REIGERSBURG CAMP	15	9 p.m.	Bn moved to REIGERSBURG CAMP. A and B Coys attached in finding sundry detachments. Beaver, straggler posts, prisoner guards and escorts	J/P43
	16	8 A.M.	Bn (less detached parties) moved to CANAL BANK Bn without 145 h.f. hole in attack on LANGEMARCK – GHELUVELT Line	J/P43
CIVILIZATION FARM		12 Noon	Bn moved forward to O.T.1 9 OG 2. Bn HQ in letter at CIVILIZATION Fm.	
	17	9 p.m.	C and D Coys relieved 4th Wores. in line, 'C' Coy taking over front line east of STEEN BEEK, 'D' Coy in support. Bn HQ at ALBERTA. From to the [?] attached parties assembled at CANAL BANK. Capt B.A.TULLIDGE killed. 2 Pts of D Coy returned to OG2	J/P43
ALBERTA	18		'A' Coy moved to OG 1 and OG 2. 'B' Coy moved from CANAL BANK to a position of readiness east of STEENBEEK	J/P43
	19	1.30 A.M.	Barrage forming up about 4 A.M. There was a heavy barrage on STEEN BEEK VALLEY and 2 Lt DOTCHAN was killed. Tanks left ST JULIEN at 4.45 A.M. and moved via ST JULIEN – TRIANGE Fm – LANGEMARCK road, firing at MASON du HIBOU th1800 from the rear. 2 Lt WILKES	J/P43

Army Form C. 2118.

WAR DIARY
or
INTELLIGENCE SUMMARY.
(Erase heading not required.)

1/8th Bn. The Worcestershire Regt.

Instructions regarding War Diaries and Intelligence Summaries are contained in F. S. Regs., Part II. and the Staff Manual respectively. Title pages will be prepared in manuscript.

Place	Date 1917	Hour	Summary of Events and Information	Remarks and references to Appendices
ROOBART CAMP	Aug 1		Heavy rain. Training impossible. Reconnaissance to KITCHENER line captured previous day.	J.P.13
"	2		Heavy rain. Training impossible	J.P.13 J.P.13
"	3		Heavy rain. Training impossible. 2 Lts H.E. PENNINGTON and J.C. HENNING joined the Bn. for duty. Former posted to 'B' Coy, and latter to 'C' Coy. Intermittent rain. A little Coy. training	J.P.13
"	4			
"	5		Church parades. 2 Lt R.N. HORSLEY rejoined the Bn. – posted to A Coy.	J.P.13
DAMBRE CAMP	6	9 AM	Bn. moved to DAMBRE CAMP – between ELVERDINGHE and VLAMERTINGHE	J.P.13 J.P.13
"	7		Coy. training	J.P.13
"	8	3 PM	Bn. moved to camp at A.30 central, about 3 miles east of POPERINGHE	J.P.13
BRAKE CAMP	9		Coy. training	J.P.13 J.P.13
"	10		Coy. training	J.P.13
"	11		Coy. training. Role Conference for Bn. Staff and Coy. Commanders.	J.P.13
"	12		Church parade.	J.P.13

32

Army Form C. 2118.

WAR DIARY
or
INTELLIGENCE SUMMARY.

(Erase heading not required.)

1/8th Bn. The Worcestershire Regt.

Instructions regarding War Diaries and Intelligence Summaries are contained in F. S. Regs., Part II. and the Staff Manual respectively. Title pages will be prepared in manuscript.

Place	Date	Hour	Summary of Events and Information	Remarks and references to Appendices
ALBERTA	19 (cont'd)		in command of "B" Coy ordered a platoon forward which captured and consolidated MAISON du HIBOU. During a number of small TRIANGLE Pns were left and consolidated and the concrete building E. & S.E. of MAISON du HIBOU. The Garrison of the Crown trench at the apex of THE TRIANGLE were taken and consolidated.	S.P.A.
			In all about 20 enemy were killed, 12 prisoners and a light MG captured.	
		4.30	A Coy relieved "C" Coy and took over HILLOCK Pn from 142nd Inf Bde.	S.P.A.
	20	4 AM	3 Pts of "C" Coy returned to OG 1 & OG 2	
		9 PM	The remaining Pts of "C" Coy returned to OG 1 & the remainder of "B" Coy handed over to 1/6 Glou and moved back to CANAL BANK.	
CANAL BANK			In a Casualties suffered during tour 1 officer & 19 OR killed, 2 officer wounded and 85 OR wounded. Consolidation complete.	S.P.A.
RUCCERSBURG CAMP	21	5 PM	Bn moved to REIGERSBURG CAMP	S.P.A.
CAMP	22		Day spent in cleaning up	S.P.A.
	23		Kitchen ceremonial and tactical training	S.P.A.
	24		Bn furnished 4 Coy working party at OG 1 & OG 2 at 12.15 P.M.	S.P.A.

Army Form C. 2118.

WAR DIARY
or
INTELLIGENCE SUMMARY.
(Erase heading not required.)

1/8th Bn. The Worcestershire Regt.

Instructions regarding War Diaries and Intelligence Summaries are contained in F.S. Regs., Part II. and the Staff Manual respectively. Title pages will be prepared in manuscript.

Place	Date	Hour	Summary of Events and Information	Remarks and references to Appendices
REIGERSBURG CAMP ALBERTA	25	9 P.M	'D'Coy moved to relieve right Coy of 1/4th Glos. in the line, arriving and coming of 2Lt J.T. Hill wounded. of 2Lt. 1/4th Wore. Rgt. 2Lt. J.T. HILL wounded. A & B Coys - training and organization of rations.	SP93
REIGERSBURG CAMP ALBERTA	26	9 P.M	Bn HQ & A & B Coys moved from camp to the line, and 'C'Coy fm OC. 2 at 9.45 P.M.. The Coys forming up in assembly trenches between HILLOCK Fm and TRIANGLE FARM. In HQ at ALBERTA. It rained and the trenches in which the men had to await zero hour were about eighteen inches deep in mud and water.	SP93
MAISON du HIBOU	27	5 AM	Bn HQ moved forward to MAISON du HIBOU.	SP93
		1.55 AM	Barrage opened along our front. The lined up close of the assembly trenches, and advanced under the barrage firing at the enemy who could be seen holding shell hole positions. The advance on the right was checked, as SPRINGFIELD was not taken by troops on right; and heavy machine gun fire from there and from the concrete emplacement north of it hampered the advance of our left. Capt TULLIDGE, 2Lt HORSLEY 2Lt J.G. HENNING were killed, and 2Lt's WILKES, MYHILL & CLARKE	

Army Form C. 2118.

WAR DIARY
or
INTELLIGENCE SUMMARY.

(Erase heading not required.)

1/8th Bn. The Worcestershire Regt.

Instructions regarding War Diaries and Intelligence Summaries are contained in F. S. Regs., Part II. and the Staff Manual respectively. Title pages will be prepared in manuscript.

Place	Date	Hour	Summary of Events and Information	Remarks and references to Appendices
MAISON du HIBOU	27		Our left were held up by some concrete emplacements about 250 yds east of LANGEMARCK – GHELUVELT line from which the enemy maintained a heavy machine gun fire. No further advance during the day. 'A' Co had suffered but little progress. 'B' and 'D' Coy came up in support. They attacked 2Lt RYAN BELL developed a flank attack on the SPRINGFIELD pill box and captured it at 6.45 P.M. 2Lt RYAN BELL was wounded (died of wounds 30.9.17) 'A' Coys were then in close support to our line which was about 150 yds east of THE TRIANGLE.	J.P.O
	28	12.30AM	'A' Coy (infantry) endeavoured to advance and take over our position to assemble at DAMBRE CAMP where relieved	J.P.O
		5AM	Bn HQ returned to MAISON du HIBOU where 'A' Coy, 'D' Coy, a party attached half to 'B' & 'C' Coys had assembled. During the night the remainder of 'B' & 'C' Coys returned to DAMBRE CAMP. Casualties for two days :— killed 3 officers, about 39 OR; Wounded 4 officers 192 OR (incl duty) missing 3 OR.	
	29	10AM	Left the scene of operations. Those who had returned from the trenches during the heading night to be marched to VLAMERTINGHE STA, entrained for HOPOUTRE detraining there and marching to SCHOOLS CAMP via ST JAANS TER BIEZEN reached at 1PM. The party that	J.P.O

(A3092) Wt W1299/M1293 75,000 1/17. D. D. & L., Ltd. Forms/C.2118/14.

35

Army Form C. 2118.

WAR DIARY
or
INTELLIGENCE SUMMARY.
(Erase heading not required.) 1/8th Bn. The Worcestershire Regt.

Place	Date	Hour	Summary of Events and Information	Remarks and references to Appendices
ST JANS TER BIEZEN	29		Bn returned from trenches during preceding night and by lorries. Patrols sent out to reinforcement camp formed on following reinforcement officers :- Capt K. HYNE, Lieut H.G.C. CARTER, 2Lts C.A. FLETCHER, W.B. BULLOCK, H.G. HIGHAM, A. ALDRICH, W.S. GUNDRY. 2Lt FLETCHER posted to 'B' Coy, 2Lt BULLOCK to 'C' Coy, 2Lt HIGHAM to 'C' Coy.	Appx
	30		Re-organisation	Appx
	31		Physical training, etc.	Appx

Major
Commanding 1/8th Bn. The Worcestershire Regt.

Confidential 14/48 Vol 30

War Diary
of
1/5th Bn the Wiltshire Regt. T.F.

From 1/9/14 to 30/9/14

(Vol XXX)

36

Army Form C. 2118.

WAR DIARY 1/8th Bn. The WORCESTERSHIRE REGT.
INTELLIGENCE SUMMARY
(Erase heading not required.)

Instructions regarding War Diaries and Intelligence Summaries are contained in F.S. Regs., Part II. and the Staff Manual respectively. Title pages will be prepared in manuscript.

Place	Date	Hour	Summary of Events and Information	Remarks and references to Appendices
SCHOOL CAMP (27 NE. 59.) "Eq.59."	1.9.17		Companies at the disposal of Company Commanders for training. 2nd Lieut. A.R. WATSON reported for duty from 2/7th Bn. The WORCESTERSHIRE REGT. 2nd Lt. A. ALDRIDGE reported for duty from 5th Army Musketry Camp	J.S.P.3
"	2.9.17		Voluntary services. Each Coy. did one hours physical training under Coy. arrangements.	J.S.P.3
"	3.9.17		Companies at the disposal of Company Commanders for training.	J.S.P.3
"	4.9.17		" " " " " "	J.S.P.3
"	5.9.17		" " " " " "	J.S.P.3
"	6.9.17		Bn. paraded for training under Bn arrangements on Training Area N.E. of ST. JAN DER BIEZEN. Lt. Col. H.A. CARR D.S.O. took over command of the 144th Inf. Bde. from Brig. Gen. H.R. DONE D.S.O. who proceeded on leave. 2nd Lt. L. McLEAN reported for duty from 46th I.B.D.	J.S.P.3
"	7.9.17		Companies at the disposal of Coy. Commanders for training.	J.S.P.3
"	8.9.17		W.O. N.C.O. and eight men per company from each Bn. of the 144th Bde. paraded on the Bde. Parade ground and were addressed by Major-General Sir R. FANSHAWE, K.C.B., who presented the "FANSHAWE CUP" to the 1/7th Bn. the WORCESTERSHIRE winners of the 48th Div. Football Competition. Bn. Sports were held in the afternoon followed by a concert.	J.S.P.3
"	9.9.17		Voluntary Services. Each Coy. did Physical Training under Coy. arrangements.	J.S.P.3
"	10.9.17		Training under Bde. arrangements on Training area.	J.S.P.3
"	11.9.17		Training under Coy. arrangements.	J.S.P.3

Army Form C. 2118.

WAR DIARY
or
INTELLIGENCE SUMMARY

1/8th Bn. the WORCESTERSHIRE REGT.

(Erase heading not required.)

Instructions regarding War Diaries and Intelligence Summaries are contained in F. S. Regs., Part II. and the Staff Manual respectively. Title pages will be prepared in manuscript.

Place	Date	Hour	Summary of Events and Information	Remarks and references to Appendices
SCHOOL CAMP	12.9.17		Training under Coy. Arrangements.	JC/13
	13.9.17		" " " " "	JC/13
	14.9.17		Training under Bn. Arrangements on Training Ground.	CE/13
	15.9.17		Training under Coy. Arrangements.	JC/13
	16.9.17		Church Parade.	JC/13
	17.9.17		Bn. moved to find Training Area at RECQUES (27 A.N.E. 1.20. 0.00 J.10.c) Bn. Left SCHOOL CAMP at 11 a.m. and marched to ABEELE STATION (B.EL. + FR. 27 N.E. L.32.6.85) Companies at 200 yds distance where it entrained. Bn. detrained at AUDRUICQ (27 A.N.E. D.10.c) and marched to RECQUES.	JC/13
RECQUES	18.9.17		Bn. arrived at RECQUES and was reported present in billets at 7 am. Bn. took part in Bde. attack according to 48th Div. Scheme on Training Area.	JC/13
	19.9.17		Bn. fired on field firing range, according to 48th Div. Scheme. Lieut Col. H.A. EARR, D.S.O. gave up command of the Bn. on temporarily taking over command of the 5th Bn. the MANCHESTER REGT. Lieut Col. A.E. CRONSHAW, T.D. from the 7th Bn. the MANCHESTER REGT. assumed Command of this battalion.	JC/13
	20.9.17			JC/13
	21.9.17		Bn took part in Divisional attack on training area according to 48th Div. ans Scheme.	
	22.9.17		Bn. fired range practices on rifle range.	JC/13
	23.9.17		Church Parade.	JC/13
	24.9.17		Training under Coy. Arrangements.	JC/13
	25.9.17		" " " " "B" Coy represented the Bn. at Div Field Firing Competition.	JC/13
	26.9.17		Training under Coy. Arrangements.	JC/13

38

WAR DIARY 1/8th Bn th WORCESTERSHIRE Regt.

INTELLIGENCE SUMMARY

Place	Date	Hour	Summary of Events and Information	Remarks and references to Appendices
RECQUES	27.9.17		Bn took part in Bde. attack according to 48th Div. Scheme.	J.S.93.
	28.9.17		Training under Coy. arrangements.	JP43
	29.9.17		" "	JP43
	30.9.17		Church Parade.	JP13
			The following decorations were awarded during the month :—	
			D.C.M.	
			Sergt. W.H. WHEELER.	
			Pte. F. TAYLOR.	
			Bar to Military Cross.	
			2nd Lt. S.H. WILLIS.	
			Military Cross.	
			2nd Lt. J.R. WILLIS	
			MILITARY MEDAL	
			Sergt. R.H. WARREN.	
			L/Sergt. F. BIRCH.	
			Cpl. H. NORLEDGE.	
			" A.N. TURNER.	
			L/C. A.T. SMITH.	
			Pte. C.A. CLAY.	
			" R. WHILEY	
			" A. CORBETT	
			" W. WILLIAMS	
			" C.F. RICE.	

J. Pleate
Major Commanding
1/8th Bn. The Worcestershire Regt.

Confidential

1/8th Worcestershire Regiment

WAR DIARY

1st October – 31st October 1917

VOLUME XXV

1/8th Bn. The WORCESTERSHIRE REGT.

Army Form C. 2118.

WAR DIARY
or
INTELLIGENCE SUMMARY.
(Erase heading not required)

Place	Date 1917	Hour	Summary of Events and Information	Remarks and references to Appendices
RECQUES	Oct. 1	2.30 a.m.	The Bn. moved from RECQUES (HAZEBROUCK 5″ 2.5 – 56.33) Nomenclature Bn. (moved at 2.30 am and entrained to AUDRUICQ. HQ"13, "D" Coy entrained at 8.30 am and detrained at VLAMERTINGHE (28 N.W. H9 a+b) H.Q.1 & "B" Coy. marched to "A" Brake Camp (28 N.W. A30 central) "D" Coy marched to REIGERSBURG CAMP (H6 b 35) from where it moved later to SPOT FARM (C12 b 33) returning to REIGERSBURG CAMP the following morning. "A" company followed on in record of personnel train and arrived at BRAKE CAMP [crossed out] the following morning. "C" company returned embarking party at PESELHOEK (26 b 29) rejoined camp late on the night of the 1/10/17.	H46
	2nd		Companies at the disposal of company commanders. "D" coy. continued with work at SPOT FARM.	H46
	3rd		"D" Coy rejoined Bn. at BRAKE CAMP. Baths allotted by the Bn. Inspection Working parties by C.O. & M.O. in northern tunnel at SPINT refuge for working party. "A" Coy & "D" Coy dutailled at forestry B.1 Sept 1 x 19 on permanent in the CANAL BANK (C25). "C" Coy found 1 officer & 4 pioneers for Brickfields leaving at HUNTER MCN. DU HIBOU (C6 c 23). Companies at the disposal of company commanders.	H46
BRAKE CAMP	4th			H46
	5th	2.30 pm	Bn. marched to DAMBRE CAMP (B 27 bent.5a)	H46
	6th		Companies at the disposal of company commanders.	H46

Army Form C. 2118.

1/8th Bn. The WORCESTERSHIRE REGT.
WAR DIARY
or
INTELLIGENCE SUMMARY.
(Erase heading not required.)

Place	Date 1917	Hour	Summary of Events and Information	Remarks and references to Appendices
CANAL BANK	Oct. 7th		The Bn marched to CANAL BANK and spent the remainder of the day preparing for the attack.	Att 16
	8th	9.30 pm	Bn marched to the SPRINGFIELD-VANCOUVER AREA (28.N.W. C.17.d.) Bn. H.Q. at SPRINGFIELD. Coys. dug in N.B. SPRINGFIELD, D & B Coys in front A & C about 150 yards in rear. Bn in position at 1.35 a.m.	Att 16
SPRINGFIELD	9th	5.20 a.m.	Att A/ Bde. a disposed on a three Bn front. (For details see Appendix A)	Appendix A. Att 16
	10th		A + D Coys were withdrawn from the front line to support positions occupied in SPRINGFIELD-VANCOUVER AREA on Y day. B Coy held the front on the front of the 1/7 WORCS. C Coy relieved at A + D Coys.	
		11.30 pm	The Bn was relieved by the 10th Bn. Pr. ARGYLE + SUTHERLAND HIGHLANDERS, who took over our dispositions at SPRINGFIELD. On being relieved the Bn proceeded by buried track to IRISH FM. (C.27. a.26) where hot coffee was waiting with two 2nd Lt. N. TINSON + 2nd Lt. INMISTON returned for duty from 46 I.B.D.	Appendix A. Att 16
	11th		Spent the morning of the day in all Coy commanders for a disposal of myselves. At 3.30 from the Battalion marched to SCHOOLS CAMP, ST JANS (N.9.d) SIEGE CAMP I marched to SCHOOLS CAMP, ST JANS	Att 16
SIEGE CAMP.	12th		TER BIEZEN. Boundaries between Companies Roads as follows BRIDGE JUNCTION, HOSPITAL FARM, DIRTY BUCKET CORNER, SWITCH ROAD,	

Army Form C. 2118.

1/8th Bn. WORCESTERSHIRE REGT.
WAR DIARY or INTELLIGENCE SUMMARY.
(Erase heading not required.)

Instructions regarding War Diaries and Intelligence Summaries are contained in F. S. Regs., Part II. and the Staff Manual respectively. Title pages will be prepared in manuscript.

Place	Date 1917	Hour	Summary of Events and Information	Remarks and references to Appendices
	Oct 12th		along POPERINGHE – ELVERDINGHE RD, SWITCH RD, POPERINGHE–WATOU RD. Rain fell heavily during the whole of the march. Lt.Col. A.E. CRENSHAW T.D. took over command of the Bn. from Major J.P. ISBATE M.C. who had command at the Bn. during operations. The following officers reported to the Bn. from VIII Corps Reinforcement Camp: Major H.T. CLARKE, Capt C.R. PAVEY M.C., 2nd Lieut. H.E. PENNINGTON. The following officers reported for duty from VIII Corps Reinforcement Camp: A. 2nd GODYEAR, 2nd Lt. TYLER, 2nd Lt. WATKINS, 2nd Lt. DREWITT, 2nd Lt. STEVENS.	H46
ROCKS CAMP.	13th		Companies at the disposal of supervising commanders for inspections and re-organisation. Major H.T. CLARKE assumed command of the Bn. Lt.Col. A.E. CRENSHAW having proceeded on leave. 2 Lt. GREENAWAY reported for duty from 46 I.B.D.	H46
	14th	1.30 am	An Australian Battalion (from ?) entrained leaving from Camp to ST. JANS TER BIEZEN and marched to HOPOUTRE Station, SN. 8 POPERINGHE. Whilst en route for train last had war-ranged to 10 p.m. At 4 pm the Bn. (LESS details ent at LIGNY ST FLOCHEL (LENS 11 G.25 - 50.22) and marched to PENIN (LENS 11 C.29 - 50.20) where it was billeted for the night.	H46
PENIN.	15th		Bn. employed in cleaning from bi– on cross roads N.E. of PENIN and marched to VILLERS AU BOIS (36 B/3 × 19) where Bn. was accommodated in SUGINEAU CAMP. R.S. MILLER reported for duty from 46 I.B.D.	H46

(A7091. Wt. W1289/M1293. 75,000. 1/17. D. D. & L., Ltd. Forms/C.2118/14.

1/8th Bn. 1/4 WORCESTERSHIRE Regt.

WAR DIARY
INTELLIGENCE SUMMARY

Army Form C. 2118.

Place	Date	Hour	Summary of Events and Information	Remarks and references to Appendices
VILLERS AU BOIS	Oct. 16th		Companies at the disposal of Company Commanders for inspections. Baths held allotted to the battalion.	A+16.
	17th		Bn. relieved 27th Bn. CANADIAN INFANTRY in trenches N.E. of VIMY. Relief complete at 12.15 a.m.	Appendix A+16. B. A+16. B.
	18th		Bn. improved trenches. Patrols sent out during the night. Hostile Artillery quiet.	A+16.
	19th		Support & DANGER reported positively from 46. I3.D. Bn. improved trenches. Patrols sent out during the night. Hostile Artillery quiet.	A+16.
	20th		Bn. improved trenches. Patrols sent out during the night. Hostile Artillery quiet.	A+16.
	21st		Bn. relieved by 1/6th GLOUC. Relief complete 9.45 p.m. During the relief the enemy put down a barrage on our support trenches and communications, on trenches which lasted about an hour. There were no casualties. On relief Bn. marched to CELLAR CAMP, NEUVILLE ST VAAST (57c NW A3) 2/Lt. BLACKER reported for duty from 46 I3D.	Appendix C A+16.
CELLAR CAMP	22nd		Companies at the disposal of Company Commanders.	A+16.
	23rd		Bn. supplied working parties for work in Camp under R.E. Baths allotted.	A+16.
	24th		Bn. supplied working parties for work on Camp under R.E.	A+16.
	25th		Bn. relieved 1/7th WORCS in support. Relief complete at 9.20 p.m.	Appendix D A+16.

Army Form C. 2118.

1/8th & 13th Bn. Worcestershire Regt.

WAR DIARY
or
INTELLIGENCE SUMMARY.
(Erase heading not required)

Instructions regarding War Diaries and Intelligence Summaries are contained in F. S. Regs., Part II. and the Staff Manual respectively. Title pages will be prepared in manuscript.

Place	Date	Hour	Summary of Events and Information	Remarks and references to Appendices
ZOLLERN HOUSE	1917 Oct. 26th		A & C Coys each provided two officers and fifty men for wiring the front line. B Coy provided one officer & fifty O.R. for carrying material to the front. D Coy furnished an officer & fifty men for work under the orders of O.C. front line Bn.	JH 16
	27th		Working parties as before.	JH 16
	28th		Working parties as before. 2nd Lieut SMITH, U.S.R. attached to the Bn for instructions for three days.	JH 16 Appendix
	29th		Bn relieved 1/7th WORCS. in trenches N.E. of Vimy. Relief complete 8.50 p.m. The 1/4 Gloucs. took over support position. Bn sent out patrols during night.	JH 16 E
	30th		Artillery rather active during the morning, but quiet during rest of day. Patrols sent out during the night. The moon was very brilliant and 2nd Lt WHISTON was wounded by M.G. bullet while on patrol. Later 2nd Lt STEVENS was wounded by M.G. bullet also while on patrol. He died of wounds the same night.	JH 16
	31st		Hostile artillery quiet during the day. Patrols sent out during the night.	JH 16
			During the month the Bn suffered the following casualties :— YPRES SECTOR : Killed Lieut. a/Capt. H.S. BENJAMIN, 2nd Lt. C.J. BEACHAM and 15 other ranks.	

Army Form C. 2118.

1/8th Bn. Worcestershire Regt.
WAR DIARY
or
INTELLIGENCE SUMMARY.
(Erase heading not required.)

Place	Date	Hour	Summary of Events and Information	Remarks and references to Appendices
	1917 Oct 31		WOUNDED:- 2nd Lt. H.G. HIGMAN and 85 other ranks. MISSING: 5 other ranks. WOUNDED + MISSING: 4 other ranks. VIMY SECTOR KILLED: 2nd Lt. R.W. STEVENS. WOUNDED: 2nd Lt. A. WHISTON and 1 other rank. The following awards were made during the month for gallantry & devotion to duty during the attack of the 9th Oct.	H.Y.G. H.Y.G. H.Y.G.

240499 Sergt. OSBORNE, J.G. — MILITARY MEDAL
242564 Pte. MARCHMENT, E.J. — "
240110 "   STYLER H.J.   — "
240291 "(A/Cpl) WOOD, H.   — "
240083 "   WESTON A.E.   — "
260022 "   PERRY A.W.   — "

H.Y. Clarke   Major.
Commanding 1/8th Bn. The Worcestershire Regt.

1/8th Bn. The Worcestershire Regt.

APPENDIX A¹. <u>Relief Orders</u>   <u>Secret</u>

1. The Battalion will be relieved by the 10th ARGYLE & SUTHERLAND HIGHLANDERS.

2. A Coy. will be relieved by the last Coy. of the A. & S.H. to arrive.

3. On relief A Coy. followed by D Coy. will proceed by TRENCH BOARD TRACK to IRISH FARM.

4. Cookers will be at IRISH FARM & hot food will be issued.

5. As soon as hot food has been issued O.C. Coys. will report to Adjutant for further orders as to time of leaving IRISH FARM. After leaving IRISH FARM Coys. will proceed to SIEGE CAMP.

6. Guide posts will be at 2A BRIDGE and at entrance to DAMBRE CAMP.

7. Lewis Guns: Their limbers will be at ADMIRALS RD. at junction

of SPRINGFIELD TRACK.

8. Hot tea will be ready on arrival at SIEGE CAMP.

10/10/17

R. ????? Capt. - Adjt.
1/8 Bn th. WORCESTERSHIRE

www.ingramcontent.com/pod-product-compliance
Lightning Source LLC
Chambersburg PA
CBHW081537160426

43191CB00011B/1779